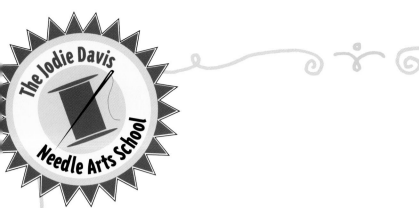

Teach Yourself to Make Angels & Fairies

Teach Yourself to Make Angels & Fairies

Simple Techniques and Patterns for Dolls and Their Clothes

Jodie Davis

Photography by Bill Milne

FRIEDMAN/FAIRFAX

PUBLISHERS

A FRIEDMAN/FAIRFAX BOOK

© 1996 by Michael Friedman Publishing Group, Inc.

Library of Congress Cataloging-in-Publication data available upon request.

ISBN 1-56799-370-2

Editor: Francine Hornberger
Art Director: Lynne Yeamans
Designer: Elan Studio
Photography Director: Christopher C. Bain
Production Associate: Camille Lee
Illustrator: Barbara Hennig

Color separations by HBM Print Ltd.
Printed in China by Leefung-Asco Printers Ltd.

Every effort has been made to present the information in this book in a clear, complete, and accurate manner. It is important that all instructions be carefully followed as failure to do so could result in injury and the publisher and the author expressly disclaim any and all liability resulting therefrom. The author also suggests refraining from using glass, bead, or button eyes on dolls intended for small children.

For bulk purchases and special sales, please contact:
Friedman/Fairfax Publishers
Attention: Sales Department
15 West 26th Street
New York, New York 10010
(212) 685-6610 • FAX (212) 685-1307

Visit the Friedman/Fairfax Website:
http://www.webcom.com/friedman

To Dad and Jayne

Contents

Introduction

Teach Yourself To Make Angels & Fairies is a dollmaking class in a book. Anyone possessing basic sewing skills will easily be able to make any of the first few dolls in this book, and by the end, will be ready to tackle most any cloth doll pattern.

How To Use This Book

I designed this book in a learn-as-you-go fashion. The first chapter covers a few of the basic skills you will need to begin making cloth dolls. I have provided a list of the basic equipment and supplies you will need, and a repertoire of basic doll-making instructions to get you started.

After reading the first chapter, you'll be able to jump right into creating any of the dolls in chapters two, three, or four. These are quick and easy dolls, requiring just a few pattern pieces and very little sewing. Each of these projects will teach you the basics of marking and stitching a doll, wigging, and making a face. Make several of these dolls to decorate wreaths, walls, Christmas trees, packages, and to give away as gifts!

The next two chapters feature more complicated doll patterns. In these chapters you will learn how to stuff cloth dolls. These projects will require more skillful sewing.

The next two chapters will each require additional skills. The variations I have provided will allow you to create numerous doll personalities.

An added bonus, the last chapter features a special teddy bear angel. Made with the skills you have learned throughout the book, this little bruin will be the perfect addition to your new collection of angels and fairies.

You will soon be feeling the magic of turning pieces of fabric and scraps of trim into loveable dolls, brimming with the personality you stitched into them. Don't forget to sign and date each doll as you finish it, and photograph the ones you'll give away. This way, you will have a chronology of all of your creations and see how your skills improve with each doll.

I look forward to having you join me in this special cloth dollmaking class! Be sure to share your dolls with me at the address you will find on page 122.

Jodie Davis

Chapter one

The Basics

This chapter focuses on the basics of dollmaking: it lists the few necessary pieces of equipment and supplies, explains preparation of patterns and fabric, and offers instruction on stuffing and face making.

Most, if not all of the items listed under equipment and supplies can be found around the house. Some items are optional, such as a glue gun, and some are used only for specific dolls. Check the instructions for the doll you are making before you begin to determine exactly which supplies you'll need.

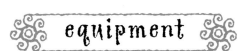

equipment

- Sewing machine
- Machine needles appropriate for the fabric used
- Dressmaker's shears
- Pinking shears
- Paper scissors
- Straight pins
- Hand sewing needles
- Dollmaker's needle (see Sources, page 123)
- Light table (optional)

supplies

- Air-soluble dressmaker's marker
- Sewing thread
- Waxed dental floss or quilting thread (for jointing)
- Polyester fiberfill stuffing
- Glue gun and glue sticks (optional)
- White tacky glue
- Fray Check or other seam sealant
- Template material: cereal boxes, Mylar, or used file folders
- #2 lead pencil
- Unlined paper
- Stuffing tools: Stuff-It (see Sources), chopsticks, wooden spoon, dowels of various sizes
- Hemostats (for stuffing and turning; see Sources)
- Face-making supplies (see page 16)

Preparing Patterns

To use the doll and clothing patterns in this book, trace the patterns onto paper or use a copy machine. If you use a copy machine, check to be sure the machine copies are accurate.

All the patterns in this book are full-size. Some were too large to fit on one page, so I cut these apart and placed them on adjacent pages. The number of parts needed to complete the pattern and the edges at which they should be joined are marked on the pieces. Follow the instructions below to use the pattern.

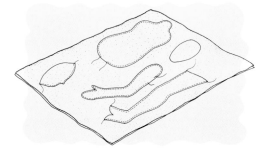

Cut out the pattern copies roughly, leaving extra paper outside the pattern lines. Glue the patterns to cereal boxes, Mylar, used file folders, or any material strong enough to withstand repeated use. With paper scissors, cut through both thicknesses along the outside edges of the pattern lines.

Preparing Fabrics

To remove sizing and fabric finishes, prewash all washable fabrics used for your doll. If you won't be laundering the doll, it's not necessary to wash any of the fabrics. Do not try to launder unusual fabrics.

Cutting Pattern Pieces

When a pattern is labeled "cut one" or "cut two" follow the instructions below for cutting the pattern pieces. Otherwise, go straight to the instructions for the doll, which will lead you through the proper process for stitching and cutting out the doll.

Place your fabric on a flat surface, smoothing it carefully. Arrange the pattern pieces on the fabric so their arrows are aligned with the lengthwise (parallel to the selvage—the lengthwise, uncut edge of the fabric) grain of the fabric. Using a #2 pencil or an air-soluble marking pen, trace the doll pattern onto the wrong side of the body fabric.

When instructed to cut two pieces of a pattern be sure to flip the pattern piece over for the second piece so you have a right and a left.

Transferring Markings

"To keep fabric from sliding as you draw on it, place a piece of sandpaper underneath."
—Linda Hershfield, Flushing, NY

To transfer simple pattern markings, such as dots, I make holes at the dots on the pattern pieces, and mark through the holes to the fabric.

For face markings I make a paper pattern, tape it to a window or place it on a light box, lay the fabric over it and draw the markings on the fabric.

Stitching

For extra-strong seams, stitch a second time on top of the first stitching. This will help prevent the seams from popping when you stuff the doll.

Try using an open-toe embroidery foot when stitching your doll. You will be able to see the marked lines as you sew along them.

"For an alternative body opening, stitch all the way around on the marked line. Overlap the beginning and end of the stitching. To turn the doll right side out, cut a slash in one layer of the doll in an area of her body which will be covered with clothing or hair."
—Brenda Groelz, Phillips, NE
—Evelyn Portrait, Lynn, MA

"Trim the seam allowances outside the stitching line with pinking shears. This method helps the fabric turn around the curves better when the body is turned right side out."
—Linda Schiffer, Columbia, MD

"Instead of making a template and tracing around it, trace the pattern directly from the book onto freezer paper. Trace the face and other markings onto the freezer paper. Iron the marked freezer paper onto the wrong side of the prepared fabric. Hold the fabric-pattern up to a light source, such as a sunny window, having the freezer paper against the window. Trace the face placement onto the right side of the fabric with a black or brown permanent pen, such as a Pigma (see Sources).

Paint, embroider, or otherwise add the features to the face.

Lay the fabric-pattern face down on a second piece of fabric which is right side up. After stitching, tear the freezer paper away from the fabric."
—Sandy Anderson, Woodbury, MN
—Joan Fearing, St. Paul, MN
—Linda Schiffer, Columbia, MD

For strong seams, set your machine's stitch length to a setting slightly shorter than the normal stitch length. Sixteen stitches per inch (2.5cm) works well for me. The smaller stitches will also make it easier to stitch around curves.

Start stitching where it is indicated on the pattern or along a straight section. Backstitch to secure the beginning of the seam.

To make sewing tight curves, such as at the neck, easier and to get better results stop after every stitch or two, leaving the needle in the fabric, and turn the fabric slightly before taking another stitch.

Backstitch at the end of the stitching.

Trimming and Clipping Seams

"To smooth the seam and give a crisp, even, finished look, insert a pointed tool such as a Stuff-It or chopstick into the doll after it is turned right side out. Run it along the seam to push it out fully and smoothly."
—Judy Rogers, Medina, OH

After stitching the doll, I trim the seam allowances to ⅛ inch (3mm). This gives the seams a smooth, finished appearance. Deeper seam allowances will not allow the fabric to give when turned and stuffed, which will cause it to pucker. Even with judicious clipping of seam allowances the finished seams often appear bumpy and uneven.

With this method I don't need to clip every curve, only sharp curves such as at the neck, and Vs such as those between the fingers.

A drop of seam sealant at these clips will prevent them from raveling. Do be careful with this product. On some fabrics it will show, even when dry, so confine it to the seam allowances. It likes to migrate, so use just a drop.

A ¼-inch (6mm) seam allowance at the unstitched opening of a body part affords more fabric for ladder-stitching the opening after stuffing the doll. To prevent fraying when ladder-stitching, apply seam sealant to the raw edges of these seam allowances.

Stuffing

To prevent a wobbly neck, insert a dowel or chopstick into the doll when stuffing from ear level to about mid-chest. For smaller dolls two coffee stirrers hot glued together may be just the right size.
—Donna Murray, South St. Paul, MN
—Kathy Samoan, Silver Spring, MD
—Judy Rogers, Medina, OH
—Marcia Spencer, Delavan, NY

"If the arms or legs are a bit lumpy after stuffing I put the part that needs smoothing between my palms and roll it as if working with clay or making a breadstick. That is often all it takes to smooth out the lumps. This works best with good-quality stuffing."
—Madeline Molis,
Rancho Palo Verdes, CA

As with most skills, stuffing is a learned art. For best results, start with high-quality stuffing. Inferior products lump in the doll and give the doll "skin" an uneven texture. Besides, lesser-quality stuffing is more difficult to work with.

Quality stuffing is resilient and will remain uniform in texture, even after pieces of varying size are stuffed into the doll. Quality stuffing costs a little more, but is a small price to pay for an easily and evenly stuffed doll. Fairfield's Soft Touch Polyfil Supreme and Airtex are my favorites.

Stuffing tools are as close as your workshop or kitchen. Cut a dowel 6 to 10 inches (15 to 25cm) long and sand one end smooth. Give the other end a point in a pencil sharpener. Sand the point smooth.

For larger dolls, the handle end of a wooden spoon works well. Chopsticks get into smaller places and are a favorite among dollmakers.

The Stuff-It™ tool has a rounded end that glides easily inside the turned body to smooth seams. It is also an excellent, sturdy stuffing tool.

Begin stuffing the smallest section of the body part first. For example, when stuffing the legs, begin with the toes. For a single-pattern-piece doll, stuff the legs, then the head, neck, and arms, and finally the torso, working toward the unstitched opening.

Size the pieces of fiberfill to the area being stuffed. For the arms and legs of a 9-inch (23cm) doll I use pieces about the size of a nickel. By the time I get to the body I use Ping-Pong-ball–size pieces. Tiny fingers require mere wisps of stuffing.

Using your stuffing tool, push the stuffing into the doll firmly. It should stay in place when you remove the tool. After you add a few more pieces, check to be sure that the first piece of stuffing is still firmly in place, filling out the fabric smoothly and firmly.

It's easy to end up with a wobbly neck, so take special care around this area, including the base of the neck and shoulders.

Aim for symmetry. If you reach the shoulder and realize the arm you just stuffed is more softly stuffed than the other arm, unstuff the second arm and start over.

You can add a small amount of stuffing to a specific spot by sliding the stuffing under the "skin" of the doll to fill a small hole. This will work only with high-quality, nonlumping stuffing.

Closing Body Seam Openings

Ladder Stitch

For a virtually invisible seam closure, use a ladder stitch.

Knot the end of a single strand of quilting thread or a double strand of sewing thread. From inside the doll, push the needle up through the fabric about 1/4 inch (6mm) below one end of the opening.

Go into the fabric close to where you came out. Come up about 1/8 inch (3mm) closer to the opening.

Take a stitch measuring about 1/8 inch (3mm) along the seamline on one side of the seam.

Cross over to the other side of the opening and take another 1/8-inch (3mm)-long stitch along the seamline, about 1/8 inch further along the opening.

Continue taking stitches from alternate sides, working your way along the opening. Pull up on the stitches as you go. When you reach the end of the opening, make a knot. Push the needle into the fabric close to the knot and emerge a short distance away. Pull the thread tight, then trim close to the fabric.

Whipstitch

If you slashed the opening to turn your doll right side out, use a whipstitch to close it. This stitch is also useful for attaching limbs (arms or legs) to the doll body.

First, apply seam sealant to the raw edges of the opening and allow to dry.

Knot the end of a single strand of quilting thread or two strands of sewing thread. Push the needle into the fabric on one side of the slash, at one end. Emerge at the other side of the slash.

Repeat along the slash, making the stitches 1/8 to 1/4 inch (3 to 6mm) apart. When you reach the end of the slash, knot and trim the thread.

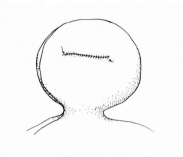

This needn't be pretty. The idea here is that the slash will be covered by hair, another body part, or the clothing of the finished doll.

Faces

Creating faces is a personal matter, one which many dollmakers find to be the most challenging aspect of dollmaking. Some dollmakers feel most comfortable with a needle, and therefore embroider. Others choose paint. Colored pencils, fabric pens, and even crayons are commonly used. You may wish to give each of these mediums a try before deciding which one you like best.

I suggest you begin by practicing on muslin scraps. As with any endeavor, practice will improve your skill.

Following is a list of supplies used for face making. You may use some or all of these.

Face-Making

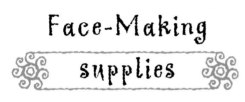

supplies

- ♥ Permanent fine-tip marking pens for drawing features (I use Pigma Microns; see Sources)
- ♥ Acrylic paints
- ♥ Textile medium (available in fabric and crafts stores)
- ♥ Paintbrushes of various sizes
- ♥ Embroidery floss
- ♥ Embroidery needles
- ♥ Colored pencils
- ♥ Makeup
- ♥ Spray fixative (available in art and craft stores)

Making Faces

More than any other detail, the face makes a doll. Some dollmakers prefer to make faces before constructing their dolls. This way, if you're unhappy with the face you made, you need only discard a piece of fabric, not a completed doll. To transfer face markings to fabric, see page 13.

Other dollmakers create faces after stitching, stuffing, and wigging the doll. I prefer this method as it gives me a frame in which to create a face, which I do freehand, rather than follow a pattern.

colorwash

Applied before painting the facial features, a wash of color tints the fabric to appear more skinlike. Colorwash can be applied as an overall coloring or to highlight specific areas, such as eyelids, shading along the nose, or cheek coloring. In the latter case I also colorwash exposed "skin" on the limbs. This technique was used for the dolls in chapter nine.

To apply a colorwash, mix textile medium with acrylic paint. Test on a scrap of the doll body fabric. The textile medium extends the color evenly, giving it a washed, rather than blotchy paint effect.

As when applying makeup, successful colorwashing involves blending. If I'm using a light brown on the face I increase the darkness a bit around the nose and eyes. After applying pink cheek color I dip my brush in plain medium, or a light brown tinted medium, and gently rub the edges of the cheek color to blend them into the skin color. If I've applied too much color I blend it out with pure medium or scrub gently with a damp paper towel while the paint is still wet.

For an antiqued look, make a batch of strong tea or coffee and paint it onto the doll. I have dunked entire rag dolls, painted (dry) face and all in tea, then left them on my sunny porch to dry.

Remember to let the colorwash dry before painting the face.

painting faces

When drawing faces, draw dots to make lines, so they won't be harsh and unnatural.

"To add a white highlight dot to the pupil of the eye, dip the tip of a toothpick or the blunt end of an unfolded paper clip into white paint. Gently apply a dot of paint to one outside edge of each pupil at two or ten o'clock."
—Linda Hargan, Elk Grove, CA

"Use a pencil point and white correction fluid for the white dots in the doll's eyes."
—Patti Welsh, Morrison, CO

Think of painting faces as a matter of layering, beginning at the bottom and working up.

I use a small brush (#0) for face painting. Toothpicks are useful for making dots or drawing tiny lines.

I usually apply two coats of paint, beginning with the whites of the eyes. When the first coat is nearly dry I add a second. Next I apply the eye color. I almost always have to mix paint to get just the right shade. Paint from the tube or jar is often too flat for a natural look. Too bright a blue might require a drop of brown, for instance, or you may have to add a dash of yellow to cheer up a dark brown.

For the second coat I like to add a little variety. For blue eyes I add tiny radiating stripes of a darker and a lighter blue. Brown eyes get darker brown and golden highlights.

When the iris is nearly dry I paint black pupils. Begin with a dot at the center and work out, enlarging it into a circle.

For the mouth, I find it easiest to paint from the inside out, otherwise it most often ends up too big. Again, paint one coat, let it dry, then paint another. Use a lighter shade along the top of the bottom lip and at the center third of the top lip. I either paint the line between the lips or draw it in with permanent pen after the paint dries.

By now the pupil should be dry. Using a toothpick or tiny brush, add two white highlights to each pupil.

Go over the eyelashes, eyebrows, and drawn lines for the eyes and nose with paint or pen.

To make freckles, dot the upper cheeks with reddish-brown paint using a toothpick or fine-tip marker.

makeup

We use makeup for our faces, so why not for our dolls' faces? I do, and I apply it the same way.

Even if I paint, embroider, or color a face with colored pencils I usually turn to powdered cosmetic blush to color the cheeks. A piece of facial

tissue is the best applicator. Wrap the tissue around your finger and dab it in the blush. Blot it and test it on a fabric scrap. Go easy with the blush. Begin with much less than you want and then build it up.

Using a fresh tissue, blend the blush into the cheek fabric, softening the edges. In addition to the cheeks, I like to apply a little blush above and between the eyebrows and to the chin.

advanced painting skills

To prevent watercolors from bleeding, apply bleedproof white—available at art supply stores—around the painted area.

For greater control when painting the small features on doll faces, use watercolor pencil.

Barbara Hennig, my artist friend and the illustrator of this book, gave me a crash course in face painting, which I'm sharing here.

Barbara told me that black doesn't exist in nature. Come to think of it, she's right. Charcoal, blue-black, brown, chestnut, and any flesh tone are fine for dolls' faces, but not black.

Likewise, look into a friend's eyes. Do you see a circle? Unless he or she is startled, the top lid covers part of the top of the circular iris.

To give the eyes a lifelike roundness, shade them in three places: the corners of the whites of the eyes,

under the top lids, and along the bottom of the iris. For the latter, use a dark shade of the color chosen for the eye color. For the lid and corner shading, use a soft gray art marker, such as the Berol Prismacolor in 10 percent Warm Gray (see Sources).

Look again at a real eye, and notice the highlights. No, there isn't a white dot at the center of the pupil. Rather, the highlight is off center, even overlapping onto the iris, and is comprised of two dots.

To help you draw lips, Barbara shares her two-over-one circle trick. She also tells me she draws the lip line before coloring the lips. To set the face so it won't smudge, spray it with a fixative, available at art and craft stores.

embroidery

Embroidered faces may be more easily executed in an embroidery hoop before the doll is cut out.

Chapter two

Linen Angel

Finished size is 15 inches (38cm) tall.

This angel is a super-easy project. Her body and arms are made of two folded lace doilies and her head is a simple oval of muslin. To vary the look, substitute embroidered tea towels or checked dish towels for the Battenburg doilies.

To display your doll, attach her to a large halolike circle to hang her as a door decoration, or set her in a wreath.

materials

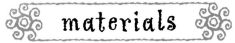

- Two 10-inch (25.5cm) square Battenburg lace doilies for dress and sleeves
- Two 6-inch (15cm) Battenburg lace heart-shaped doilies for wings
- Matching thread
- Scrap of muslin
- Small bit of stuffing
- Small amount of hair material
- ⅓ yard (30.5cm) of ¼-inch (6mm) wide ribbon

instructions

1. Fold one of the square doilies as shown. This will be the dress.

view is from front

2. Fold the second square doily almost in half with one section slightly larger than the other. Place on top of the first doily as shown, having the larger half on top, with the bottom tip of the top half extending about 1½ inches (4cm) above that of the bottom half. Fold the top tip of the dress doily over the sleeve doily. Pin together. Stitch through all layers along lace edge so the stitching won't show.

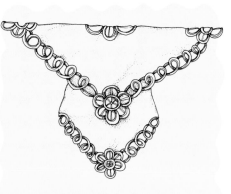

view is from front

3. Stitch the wings to the back of the doll.

4. With right sides together, stitch two head pieces together. Make a slash in one piece and turn right side out. Stuff. Whipstitch the slash closed. Stitch the head over the wings with the chin overlapping the fold at the top edge of the sleeve.

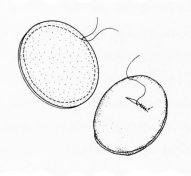

5. For face instructions, turn to pages 16–17.

6. Pull a piece of hair rather than cut it, so the end won't be blunt. Glue the hair to the head. Tie ribbons and tack one to each side of the face.

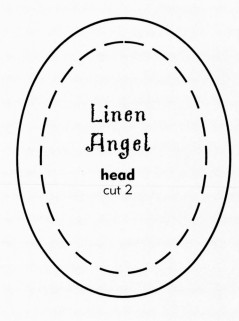

Linen Angel
head
cut 2

Chapter three

Floppy Dolls

Finished size is 9½ inches (24cm) tall.

This doll's body is simply two tubes
of fabric tied together and softy stuffed,
making the doll infinitely posable. The clothing is
simple squares of fabric embellished with scraps
of trims. Definitely a quick doll to make,
and a perfect beginner project.

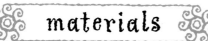 materials

Body
- ⅛ yard (11.5cm) of lightweight fleece fabric
- Matching thread
- Polyester fiberfill stuffing

Flower Sprite
- ⅛ yard (11.5cm) of satinlike fabric
- Matching thread
- ½ yard (46cm) of ruffled trim in each of two colors
- Satin roses with leaves
- ¾ yard (69cm) of ribbon for ankles and wrists (optional)
- Blonde Wavy Locks from All Cooped Up Designs (see Sources)
- ⅔ yard (61cm) of wire-edged ribbon for wings

Garden Fairy
- ⅛ yard (11.5cm) of gold lamé
- Matching thread
- ⅛ yard (11.5cm) of chiffon for ruffle
- Matching thread
- Scrap of lace for collar
- ¾ yard (69cm) of ribbon for ankles and wrists (optional)
- Gold Heavenly Hair from By Hand (see Sources)
- Narrow ribbon, preserved or silk flowers
- Beaded plastic wire loops (sold in the bridal department of crafts stores)

instructions

1 Prepare patterns and cut out fabric as instructed on page 12.

2 With right sides together, stitch the two arm pieces together, leaving an opening between the dots for turning. Trim the seam allowances around

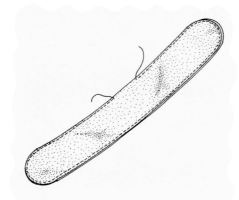

the hand to ⅛ inch (3mm). Turn arms right sides out. Stuff the hands to about ¾ inch (2cm). Tie knots at the wrists. Repeat for the legs, stuffing to about 1 inch (2.5cm). Stuff the arms and legs very softly, just enough to hold their shape, leaving about 2 inches (5cm) at the center unstuffed.

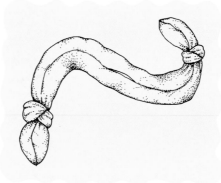

3 Tie the legs around the middle of the arms as shown, being careful to adjust the knot before tightening so the legs are of equal length.

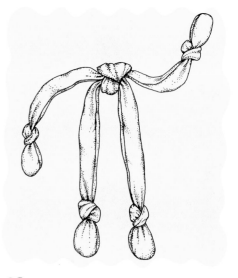

4 With right sides together, stitch the two head pieces together, leaving the straight, bottom edges unstitched. Gather the bottom edge of head. Stuff

the head softly. Pull up on the stitches and secure. Stitch the head to the knot at the intersection of the legs and arms.

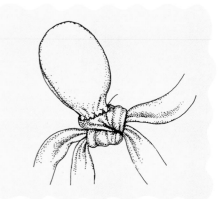

5 With right sides together, stitch the side seams of the leotard, leaving the area above the dots unstitched.

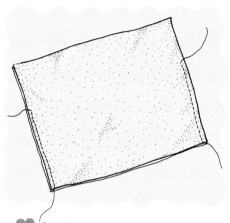

6 Put the leotard on the doll so the arms fit into these unstitched slits and the legs fall out of the center of the tube. Turn the raw edges at the unstitched slits ¼ inch (6mm) to the inside. Fold the top edge of the leotard about ¼ inch (6mm) to the inside. Baste around top edge. Pull up on the stitches to gather the leotard around the neck. Knot the thread.

7 **For Flower Sprite:** Baste around the lower edge of the leotard. Stuff the leotard softly. Pull up on the stitches to gather the leotard around the doll's legs. Knot.

Stitch ruffled trim near lower edge of leotard and around neck. Stitch roses in place.

For Garden Fairy: Cut a 2 × 22-inch (5 × 56cm) strip of chiffon. Satin stitch close to one long edge. Trim close to stitching. Cut strip in half to make two 11-inch (28cm) long pieces. With right sides together, fold each piece in half, matching the 2-inch (5cm) long edges. Stitch.

Fold ¼ inch (6mm) to the wrong side along the raw edge. Gather.

Fold the lower edge of the leotard to the wrong side. Stitch. Place one skirt layer over the bottom edge of the leotard. Pull up on the gathers to fit. Stitch. Repeat for the second skirt layer.

Sew flowers in place. From the remaining chiffon, satin stitch all around a piece measuring about 4 × 12 inches (10 × 30.5cm). Fold in half lengthwise twice. Tie into a bow. Sew bow to front of dress.

8 Tie ribbon around ankles and wrists, if desired.

9 For the Garden Fairy, cut the hair into 5-inch (12.5cm) long lengths. Draw a 1-inch (2.5cm) long line on a piece of paper. Stitch the center of the hair to the line. Tear paper from hair. Cut short pieces of hair and glue to head for bangs. Glue or stitch the hair to the head, having the seam run front to back over the bangs. Glue a flower in the hair.

When working with fine-fiber hair material, use tweezers to arrange individual wisps on the glue-covered doll head. Keep a moist paper towel or baby wipe handy to keep the tweezers free of glue.

For the Flower Sprite, glue hair to head, softly curving it around the face. Glue flowers in the hair.

10 For face-making instructions, turn to pages 16–17.

11 For Flower Sprite wings, fold the ribbon into two loops on each side. Tack loops to the back of the doll.

For Garden Fairy wings, trim the ends of the plastic bead wire and hand stitch the "wings" to the doll's back.

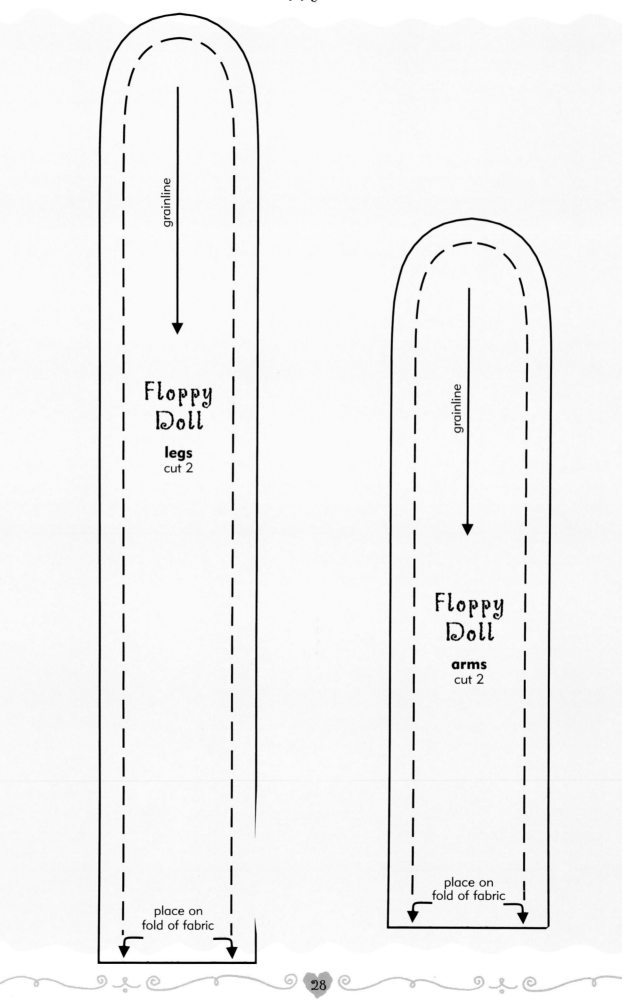

Floppy
Doll

legs
cut 2

grainline

place on
fold of fabric

Floppy
Doll

arms
cut 2

grainline

place on
fold of fabric

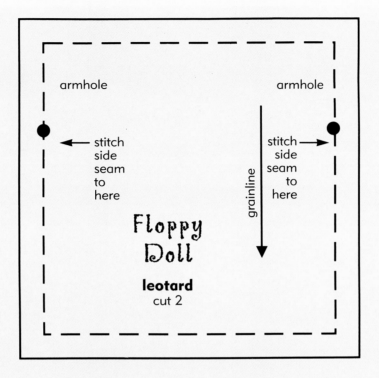

armhole   armhole

stitch
side
seam
to
here

stitch
side
seam
to
here

grainline

Floppy
Doll

leotard
cut 2

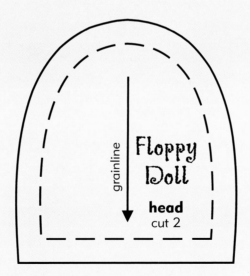

grainline

Floppy
Doll

head
cut 2

Chapter four

Dainty Angels

Finished size is 15 inches (38cm) tall.

With just arms and a head-torso, this doll is quick and easy to make. Her dress is constructed from simple pattern shapes. Instructions for three angels are provided: a Lace, Valentine, and Celestial Angel. Make the Lace Angel from white or tea-dyed lace and doilies, or, for a colorful yet delicate Lace Angel, dye the fabrics before stitching. For the Valentine Angel, cut a heart from your fabric using the pattern at the end of the chapter, or use a doily as I did.

materials
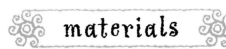

Angel Doll
- ⅛ yard (11.5cm) of muslin
- Matching thread
- Polyester fiberfill stuffing

Lace Heart Angel
- 1 yard (1m) of eyelet fabric with a finished edge
- Three 4-inch (10cm) heart-shaped Battenburg lace doilies (two for wings, one for dress)
- ⅛ yard (11.5cm) of gold braid trim for crown
- ⅛ yard (11.5cm) of long gold twisted trim for hair

Valentine Angel
- ⅓ yard (30cm) of fabric for dress
- Matching thread
- ⅔ yard (61cm) of 2½-inch (6.5cm) wide eyelet edging for lower edge of dress
- Scrap of fabric for undersleeve edgings
- ⅓ yard (30cm) of ⅜-inch (9mm) wide lace for sleeve trim
- ⅔ yard (61cm) of ribbon trim for skirt hem
- One 4-inch (10cm) heart-shaped Battenburg lace doily
- ⅓ yard (30cm) of ribbon for bow
- Assorted gold charms
- One package Auburn Wavy Locks from All Cooped Up Designs (see Sources)
- One 12-inch (30.5cm) heart doily for wings

Celestial Angel
- ⅓ yard (30cm) of fabric for dress
- Matching thread
- ¼ yard (23cm) of fabric for bow, dress, and sleeve underhem edgings
- 1 yard (1m) of rickrack
- Gold button star or charm
- Gold stars on wire
- One package Blonde Stringlets from All Cooped Up Designs (see Sources)
- ¼ yard (23cm) of fusible interfacing
- Batting
- 2 yards (2m) of 2-inch (5cm) wide wire-edged ribbon

instructions

Note: All seam allowances are ¼ inch (6mm) unless specified otherwise.

1 Prepare fabrics and patterns as instructed in chapter one. Transfer the face markings to the right side of one head piece.

Body

2 With right sides together, stitch the two head-torso pieces together, leaving the bottom edges open.

Turn right side out. Stuff to about ½ inch (12mm) from bottom opening. Machine zigzag or hand whipstitch the opening closed.

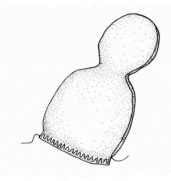

3 With right sides together, stitch the two arms together, leaving the straight edges at the shoulder unstitched. Repeat for the second set. Stuff the arms. Machine zigzag or hand whipstitch the openings closed.

4 Stitch the arms to the head-torso as shown.

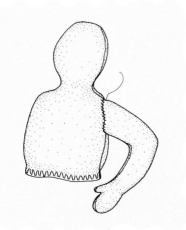

Clothing

Lace Heart Angel

♥ Cut the eyelet fabric so it measures 12 inches (30.5cm) wide above finished edge as shown. Cut piece in half across width. Set one piece aside for the skirt. Trim remaining half to 6½ inches (16.5cm) wide. Cut this piece in half for sleeves.

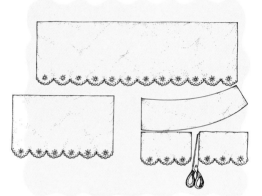

♥ With right sides together, stitch the 12-inch (30.5cm) ends together for the center back seam of the skirt. Turn skirt right side out. Center the

seam at the back of the skirt. Fold the remaining (top) raw edge of the skirt ¼ inch (6mm) to the wrong side. Gather about ⅛ inch (3mm)

below the fold through both layers. Pull up on the stitches as far as they will go. Knot to secure. Stitch

the skirt to the bottom of the head-torso.

♥ With right sides together, fold a sleeve piece in half, matching the short edges. Stitch. Gather a sleeve 1¾ inches (4.5cm) above the lower finished eyelet edge. Slip the sleeve onto the arm. Pull up on the stitches. Tie the ends of the threads in a knot.

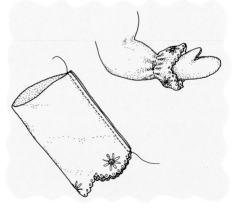

Turn the raw edge at the top of the sleeve about ¼ inch (6mm) to the wrong side. Gather folded edge and leave the needle and thread attached. Pull up on the thread to fit around the top of the arm where it is stitched to the head-torso. Hand stitch around through the sleeve and arm-body to secure. Repeat for the second sleeve.

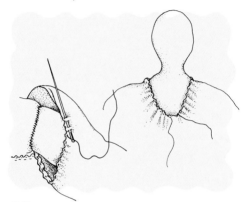

♥ Hand stitch one doily to the front of the doll.

♥ Stitch the gold twisted trim around the back and sides of the top of the doll's head. Stitch the gold braid on top, hiding the finished top edge of the twisted trim hair.

♥ Turn to pages 16–17 for face-making instructions.

♥ Stitch the two remaining doilies to the back of the doll for the wings.

Valentine Angel

💜 Cut a 12 × 22-inch (30.5 × 56cm) piece of fabric for the skirt. Cut the two sleeves from the remaining fabric.

💜 With right sides together, stitch the shorter ends together for the center back seam of the skirt. Turn skirt right side out. Press 1½ inches (4cm) to the wrong side along one raw edge. With right sides together, stitch the short ends of the hem trim together. Pin trim inside the skirt hem, matching the seams. Baste trim in place. Topstitch the ribbon trim over the basting.

Center the skirt seam at the center back of the skirt. Fold the remaining (top) raw edge of the skirt ¼ inch (6mm) to the wrong side. Gather about ⅛ inch (3mm) below the fold.

Pull up on the threads fairly tightly. Knot the thread. Stitch the skirt to the head-torso.

💜 6   With right sides together, fold a sleeve piece in half, matching the short edges. Stitch. Press under 1½ inches (4cm) along one raw edge. With right sides together, stitch the short edges of the sleeve underhem piece together. Fold as shown. Match the raw edge of the underhem piece to the raw edge of the folded undersleeve edge. Baste about ⅛ inch (3mm) below the raw edges, beginning and ending the stitching at the seam. Leave a long end of thread. Fold the remaining

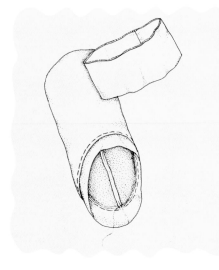

(top) raw edge of the sleeve ¼ inch (6mm) to the wrong side. Baste about ⅛ inch (3mm) from the fold. Put the sleeve on the doll. Pull up on the stitches at the top edge, gathering the edge of the sleeve around the very top of the arm. Knot thread. Hand stitch through the sleeve and arm-body to secure.

Pull up on the stitches at the lower sleeve to gather around the arm below the elbow. Knot thread. Hand sew the trim over the gathering. Repeat for the second sleeve.

💜 7   Hand stitch a doily to the front of the doll.

💜 8   Tie ribbon into a bow. Tack bow to the front of the doily. Sew the charms in place.

💜 9   Arrange the hair on the doll's head to give it a full, natural look. Make a part at the center top or just to one side of center at the top of the head. Glue hair in place.

💜 10   Turn to pages 16–17 for face-making instructions.

💜 11   Stitch or glue the doily wings to the doll's back.

Celestial Angel

💜 1   Cut a 12 × 22-inch (30.5 × 56cm) piece of fabric for the skirt. Cut the two sleeves from the remaining fabric.

💜 2   With right sides together, stitch the 12-inch (30.5cm) ends together for the center back seam of the skirt. Fold ¼ inch (6mm) to the wrong side along lower edge of skirt. Stitch the two short edges of the skirt hem piece together. Fold the skirt hem piece as shown. Press 1½ inches (4cm) to the

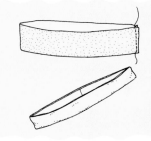

inside along one raw edge. Place the skirt hem piece under the hem of the skirt, matching raw edges and seams. Pin. Baste. Topstitch

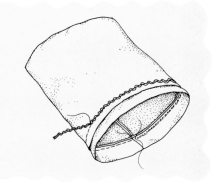

the rickrack over the basting, securing hem piece in place. Center the skirt seam at the center back of the skirt. Fold the remaining (top) raw edge of the skirt ¼ inch (6mm) to the wrong side. Gather about ⅛ inch (3mm) below the fold.

Pull up on the threads fairly tightly. Knot thread. Stitch the skirt to the head-torso.

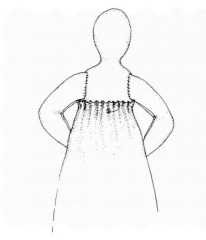

6   With right sides together, fold a sleeve piece in half, matching the short edges. Stitch. Press under 1½ inches (4cm) along one raw edge. With right sides together, stitch the short edges of the sleeve underhem piece together. Fold as shown. Match the raw edge of the underhem to the raw edge of the folded undersleeve edge. Baste about ⅛ inch (3mm) below the fold, beginning and ending the stitching at the seam edge. Leave a long end of thread. Fold the remain-

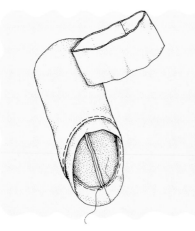

ing (top) raw edge of the sleeve ¼ inch (6mm) to the wrong side. Baste about ⅛ inch (3mm) from the fold. Put the sleeve on the doll. Pull up on the stitches at the top edge, gathering the edge of the sleeve around the very top of the arm. Knot thread. Hand

stitch through the sleeve and arm-body to secure. Pull up on the stitches at the lower sleeve to gather around the arm below the elbow. Knot thread. Hand sew the rickrack over the gather stitches. Repeat for the second sleeve.

7   Fold the bow piece so the right sides are together. Stitch, leaving a 1-inch (2.5cm) wide opening for turning. Trim seam allowances at corners.

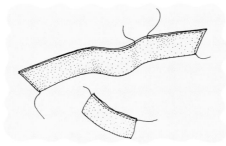

Turn right side out. Press. Fold as shown. Fold the center tie piece as shown. Fold tie over the center of the

bow, pinching the bow to gather it. Whipstitch as shown. Sew bow to the doll's front. Sew the star to the center of the bow.

view is from back

8   Remove the string from the hair. Glue the hair in one piece around the doll's head from one side of the head to the other. Glue all the way down the sides so the ends stay close to the head in curls. Do the same at the back of the head until it is covered with hair.

9   Turn to pages 16–17 for face-making instructions.

10   To make the wings, fold 2yds (1.8m) of the 2-inch (5cm) wide wire-edged ribbon into three loops. Pinch center together and hand stitch to back of doll.

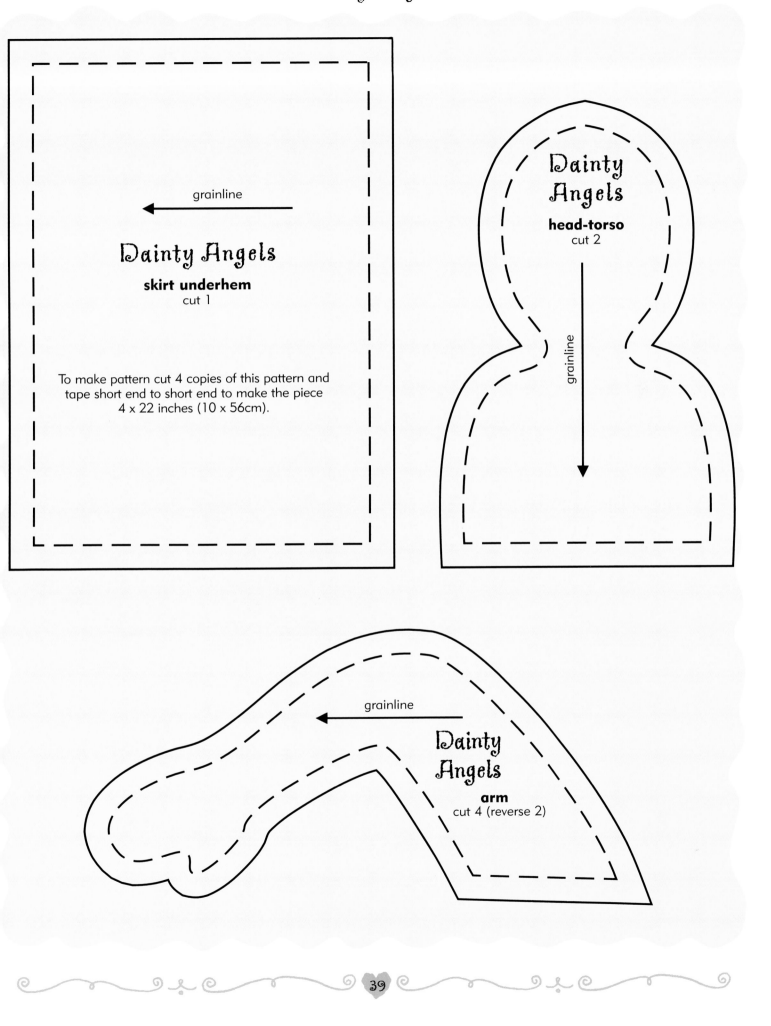

grainline

Dainty Angels

skirt underhem
cut 1

To make pattern cut 4 copies of this pattern and
tape short end to short end to make the piece
4 x 22 inches (10 x 56cm).

Dainty Angels

head-torso
cut 2

grainline

grainline

Dainty Angels

arm
cut 4 (reverse 2)

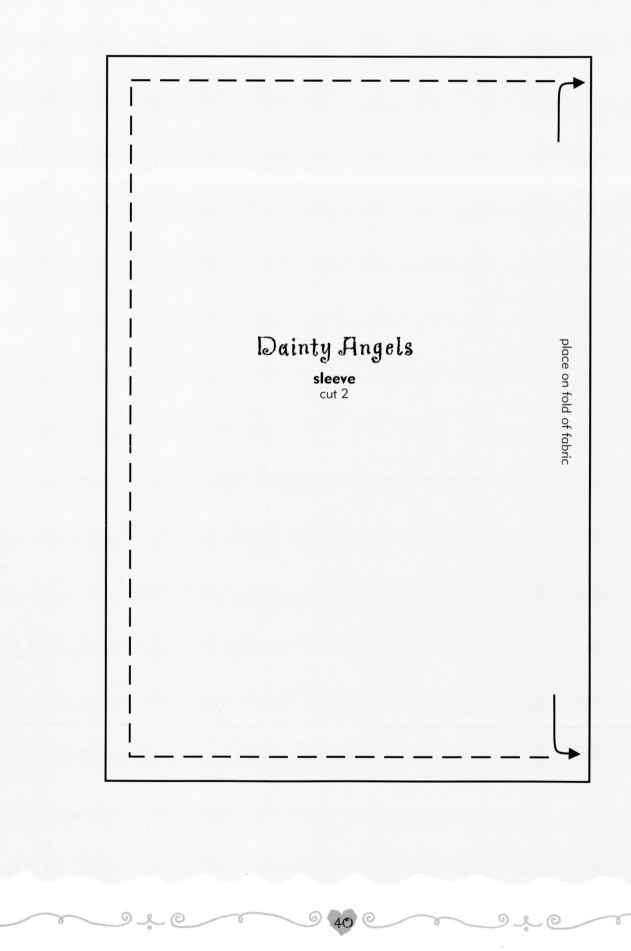

Dainty Angels

sleeve
cut 2

place on fold of fabric

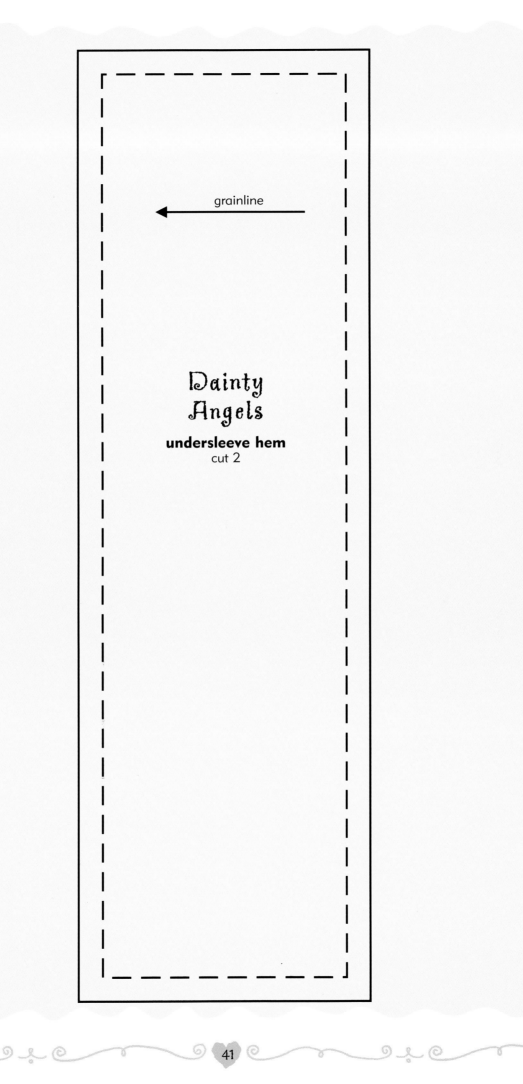

grainline

Dainty
Angels

undersleeve hem
cut 2

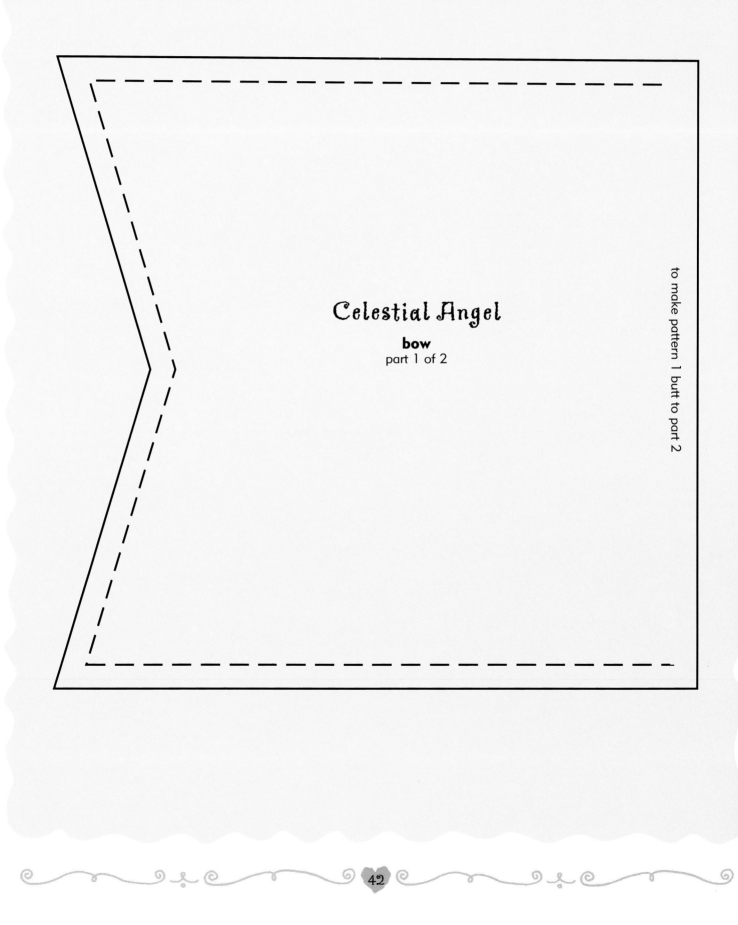

Celestial Angel

bow
part 1 of 2

to make pattern 1 butt to part 2

butt and tape to part 1

Celestial Angel

bow
part 2 of 2
cut 1

place on fold of fabric

Chapter five

Flying Angel

Finished size is 11 inches (28cm) tall.

With just one pattern piece, this doll is a snap to make. And there's no clothing to construct; it is stitched as part of her body.

an opening for turning between the dots. Cut out doll ⅛ inch (3mm) outside marked line. Turn right side out. Stuff. Ladder stitch the opening closed.

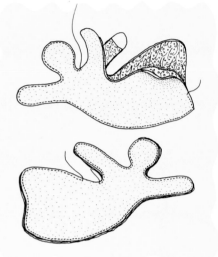

materials

- 14 × 18-inch (35.5 × 46cm) piece of muslin
- Matching thread
- 14 × 18-inch (35.5 × 46cm) piece of fabric for dress
- ½ yard (46cm) of lace trim
- Three small bells or buttons
- One package Auburn Stringlets or Auburn Wavy Locks from All Cooped Up Designs (see Sources)
- Two 4-inch (10cm) gold doily hearts or purchased wings

instructions

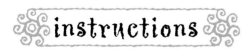

1. Prepare the patterns as instructed on page 12. Cut a second body pattern to use as a template for the dress fabric. Trim the pattern along the neck and wrist lines.

2. Fold the muslin so it measures 9 × 14 inches (23 × 35.5cm). Trace the angel pattern onto one half of the muslin by holding it up to a sunny window or light table and tracing onto the wrong side of the fabric.

3. Fold the dress fabric so the right sides are together and it measures 9 × 14 inches (23 × 35.5cm). Trace the dress template onto the fabric. Cut the fabric along the neck and wrist lines.

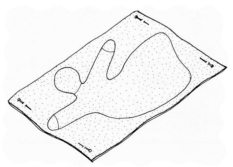

4. Put the dress fabric inside the muslin, matching the wrist and neck lines and having the marked side of the muslin facing up. Stitch just inside the line traced on the muslin, leaving

5. Hand stitch the trim over the raw edges of the fabric at the wrists and neck, and waist, if desired. Stitch trim along the bottom of the dress.

6. Stitch buttons or bells to the front of the dress.

7. For the red hair, loop the hair and glue it to the doll's head. For the brown, stringy hair, glue the string of hair around the doll's face and then fill in the back of the head. Bring the end of the hair to one side, form a loop "ponytail," and secure.

8. Apply your doll's face as instructed on pages 16–17.

9. Glue or stitch the two gold doily hearts or the purchased wings to the back of the doll.

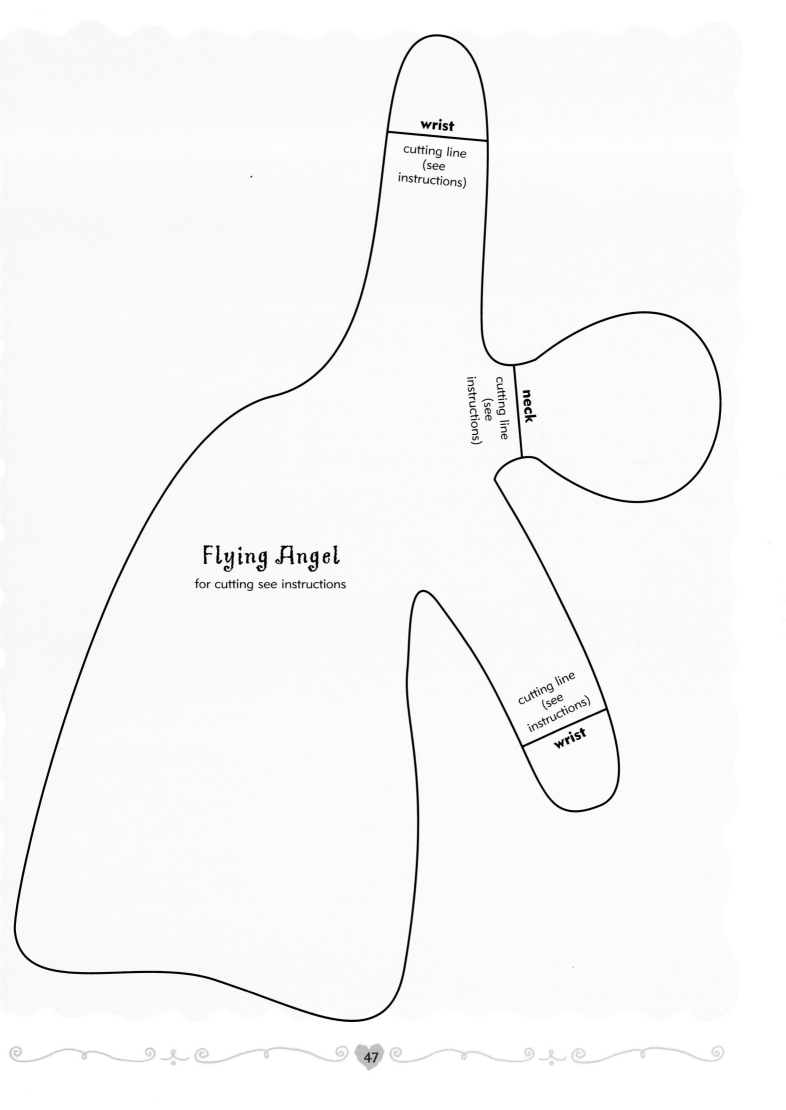

wrist

cutting line
(see
instructions)

cutting line
(see
instructions)

neck

Flying Angel

for cutting see instructions

cutting line
(see
instructions)

wrist

Chapter six

Country Angel

Finished size is 11 inches (28cm) tall.

Quick and easy to make, this witty
angel is stitched in one step: the clothing
is constructed as one with the doll body.
Make this in Christmas prints for the holidays,
or choose white or creamy off-white fabrics
for a season of fun.

materials

- ¼ yard (23cm) of muslin
- ¼ yard (23cm) of fabric for dress-upper sleeve
- Fabric scraps for sleeves and bloomer-legs
- Matching thread
- Polyester fiberfill stuffing
- ½ yard (46cm) of trim
- Waxed dental floss or quilting thread
- Four ½ to ¾-inch (12mm to 2cm) diameter buttons
- Two or three small buttons for the front of the dress (optional)
- Dark Brown Curly Locks or Blonde Stringlets from All Cooped Up Designs (see Sources)
- Two 4½-inch (11.5cm) doilies or ¼ yard (23cm) of fabric and batting for wings
- Ribbon for bow or roses on a ribbon to decorate hair

instructions

1 Prepare the patterns as instructed on page 12.

2 Trace the body pattern onto the muslin. Cut it out, leaving roughly a ½-inch (12mm) seam allowance all around. Cut a second piece approximately the same size. Place the marked piece, marked side up, on top.

Cut two 5½-inch (14cm) squares of dress-upper sleeve fabric. Lay one on top of the other, right sides together. Lift the top, marked, piece of muslin and place the dress fabric between the muslin layers, placing a straight raw edge along the neckline. Pin the layers together. Stitch just inside the marked line, leaving a ¾-inch (2cm) wide opening at one side for turning. Trim the seam allowances to ⅛ inch (3mm). Clip into the seam allowances at both sides of the neck. To prevent fraying, apply a drop of seam sealant to both these clips. Allow to dry. Turn right side out.

3 Trace the arm pattern onto muslin. Cut it out, leaving roughly a ½-inch (12mm) seam allowance around the marked line. Cut a second piece of muslin roughly the same size. Place the marked piece, marked side up, on top. Cut two 3 × 4½-inch (7.5 × 11.5cm) pieces of sleeve fabric. Lay one on top of the other, right sides together. Cut a straight line across one edge. Lift the top, marked piece of muslin and place the sleeve fabric underneath, lining up the straight cut edge along the wrist.

Pin the layers together. Stitch just inside the marked line, leaving a ¾-inch (2cm) opening in the stitching for turning and stuffing.

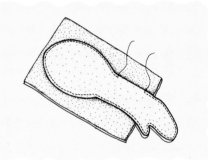

Repeat for the second sleeve. Assemble legs in the same manner, cutting two 3 × 4½-inch (7.5 × 11.5cm) pieces of bloomer-leg fabric.

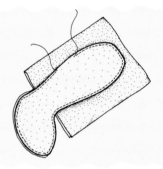

Do the same for the two thighs, covering them entirely with the bloomer-leg fabric.

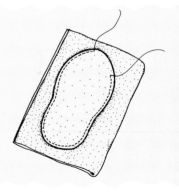

Trim the seam allowances to ⅛ inch (3mm).

6 To thread joint the doll's arms, thread a dollmaker's needle with quilting thread or waxed dental floss. Make a double knot in one end.

Insert the needle into the inside of one arm (so the thumbs face forward and up), about ⅝ inch (1.5cm) below the top of the arm. Push the needle through the sleeve fabric, through the arm, and out the other side of the arm through the sleeve fabric. Go back in the sleeve fabric on the outside of the arm into the same hole from which the needle emerged. This way the thread will be caught in the arm, not the sleeve, leaving the sleeve free.

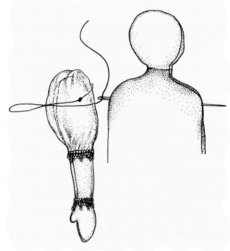

Push the needle through the arm and into the body and emerge out the other side of the body. Joint the second arm in the same manner, come back through the body, pull tight, and knot.

7 Stitch the trim over the raw edges of the fabric at the doll's ankles and wrists. Attach the lower legs to the upper legs with buttons, as shown. Stitch through buttons to attach the upper legs to the backside of the doll.

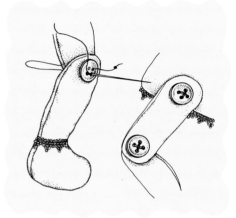

8 Stitch trim around the doll's neck, as a collar. Stitch the small buttons to the center front of the dress, if desired.

9 For the hair, glue 9-inch (23cm) lengths of hair across the doll's head. Add bangs, if desired. Glue or tack a bow to the top of her head or wind a ribbon of roses through her hair.

10 Make your doll's face as instructed on pages 16–17.

11 Glue or stitch the two doilies to the doll's back. Or, for fabric wings, fold the wing fabric so the right sides are together. Trace the wing pattern onto the folded fabric. Lay the fabric on top of the batting. Stitch just inside the marked line, leaving a 1½-inch (4cm) opening for turning. Trim the seam allowances to ⅛ (3mm). Turn right side out. Hand stitch the opening closed. Stitch or glue wings to the angel's back.

4 Turn the pieces right side out. Stuff. Ladder stitch the openings closed, as instructed on page 15.

5 Gather along the edge of a sleeve. Pull up on the stitches. Place sleeve around the top of an arm. Pull up on the stitches to fit the arm and knot. Cut a piece of sleeve bottom fabric 3½ × 4 inches (9 × 10cm). Seam the 4-inch (10cm) long edges together. Fold like the cuff of a sock so that the 3½-inch (9cm) long edges meet. Turn the raw edges to the inside. Put on doll's arm. Tack in place. Stitch a piece of trim over the top and bottom edges of the bottom sleeve.

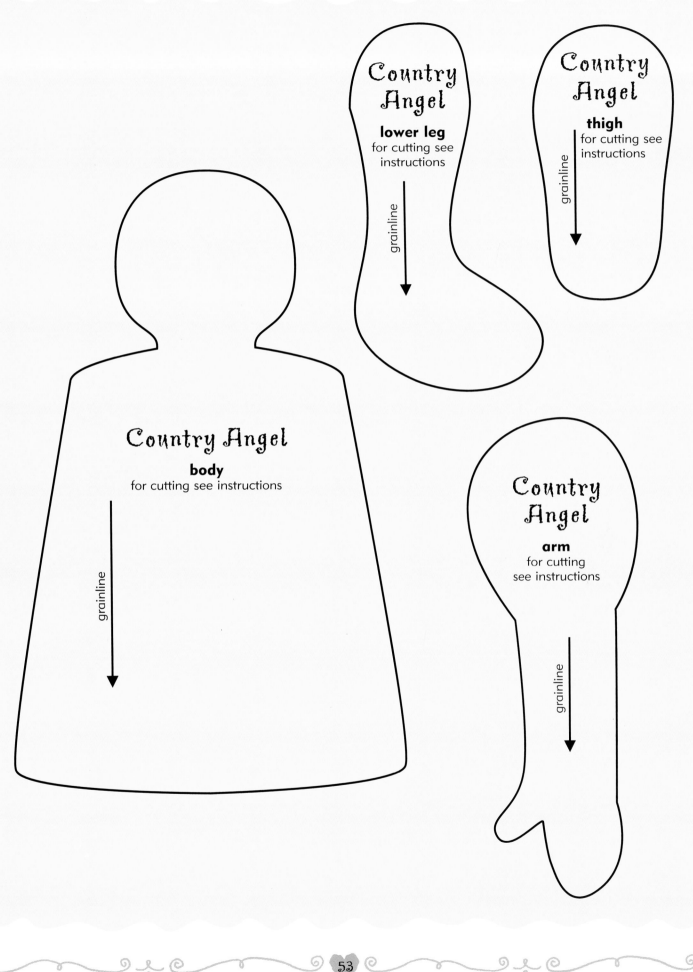

Country Angel

lower leg
for cutting see
instructions

grainline

Country Angel

thigh
for cutting see
instructions

grainline

Country Angel

body
for cutting see instructions

grainline

Country Angel

arm
for cutting
see instructions

grainline

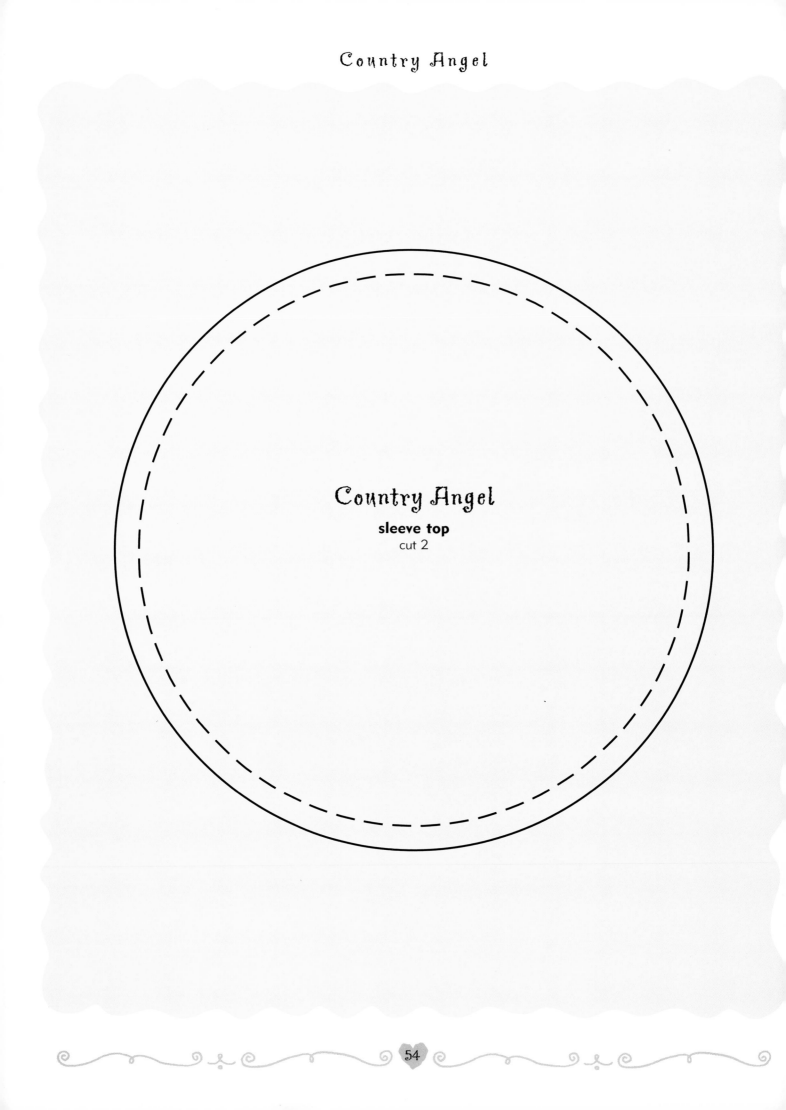

Country Angel

sleeve top
cut 2

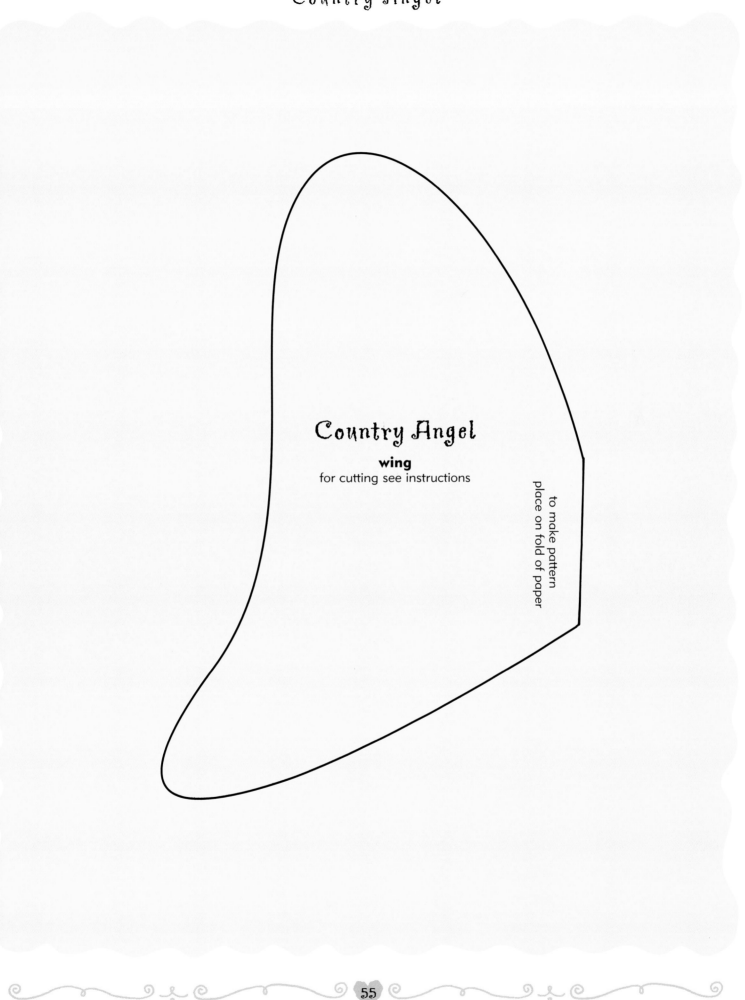

Country Angel

wing
for cutting see instructions

to make pattern
place on fold of paper

Chapter seven

Pancake Dolls

Finished sizes: Small doll is 5 inches (13cm) tall.
Large doll is 12 inches (30.5cm) tall.

The first doll in our lineup with a traditional doll body and separate clothing, this doll requires but one pattern piece for her body, thereby making her a beginner level doll. I have included patterns for dolls in two sizes.

The smaller size is just right on a wreath or as a Christmas tree ornament. Check the bridal department of your crafts store for wing possibilities for your doll.

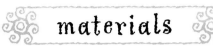

materials

Woodland Fairy
- ⅓ yard (30cm) of muslin
- Matching thread
- Polyester fiberfill stuffing
- ½ yard (46cm) of eyelet fabric
- ½ yard (46cm) of fine netting
- 1 yard of 1-inch (2.5cm) wide ribbon
- Two ⅜-inch (9mm) diameter round black buttons
- Dried flowers and leaves
- Small basket
- Two sets of white embroidered wired leaves for wings
- Butterfly
- Medium Brown Country Curls from Twice as Nice (see Sources)

Small Angels
Body
- 6 × 12-inch (15 × 30.5cm) piece of muslin
- Matching thread
- Polyester fiberfill stuffing

Clothing
Eyelet Angel
- ⅓ yard (30cm) of 3-inch (7.5cm) wide ungathered eyelet trim
- ⅓ yard (30cm) of 1-inch (2.5cm) wide lace trim with eyelets for ribbon
- ½ yard (46cm) of ⅛-inch (3mm) wide ribbon
- Two 2½-inch (6.5cm) doilies
- Medium Brown Country Curls from Twice As Nice (see Sources)

Sunflower Angel
- 4½ × 6-inch (11.5 × 15cm) piece of fabric for dress
- One 3-inch (7.5cm) doily
- One button
- Beads for eyes
- Curly Crepe Wool Hair from All Cooped Up Designs (see Sources)
- String
- Cardboard for wings

Star Angel
- 4½ × 6-inch (11.5 × 15cm) piece of fabric for dress
- Matching thread
- Yarn for hair
- Fabric scraps for hair ties and wings
- Scrap of batting
- Embroidery floss

instructions

Note: Seam allowances are ¼ inch (6mm) unless specified otherwise.

1. Prepare the patterns and fabric as instructed on page 12.

2. Using a #2 pencil or an air-soluble marker, trace the doll pattern onto the wrong side of the body fabric.

3. Lay the pattern on a light table or tape it to a sunny window. Trace the body outline and the face onto the right side of the fabric.

4. Lay the fabric right side down on a second piece of body fabric which is right side up. Pin the layers together.

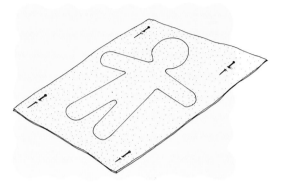

5. Backstitch to secure the beginning of the seam, then stitch just inside the traced lines. When you sew tight curves, such as at the neck, you may have to stop after each stitch to lift the presser foot and pivot the fabric slightly. Take one stitch straight across the body at the crotch. Stop stitching about ¾ inch (2cm) for the small doll or 2 inches (5cm) for the large doll before reaching the beginning of the stitching. Backstitch.

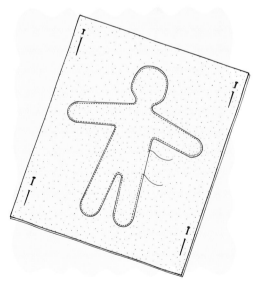

6 Cut the doll out ⅛ inch (3mm) outside the stitched line, except at the unstitched opening: trim this to ¼ inch (6mm). Clip into the curve at the neck and to the straight stitch between the legs. Apply seam sealant to the clips.

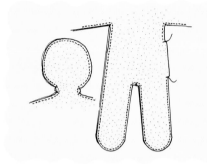

Allow to dry. Turn the doll right side out. Smooth the seams by inserting a pointed stuffing tool into the doll and running it along the seams to push them out.

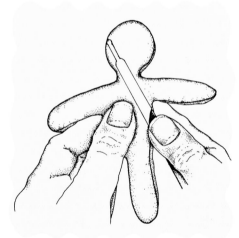

7 Stuff the doll (see page 14), beginning with the legs. Then stuff the head, neck, and arms. Finish by stuffing the torso.

8 Ladder stitch (see page 15) the gap in the stitching at the side of the doll closed.

Clothing

Woodland Fairy

1 Cut the eyelet into four pieces: two 3½ × 4 inches (9 × 10cm) for sleeves and two 3½ × 6½ inches (9 × 16.5cm) for the dress-bodice.

2 With right sides together, fold a sleeve in half. Stitch the raw edges together. Turn right side out. Put on doll. Repeat for other sleeve.

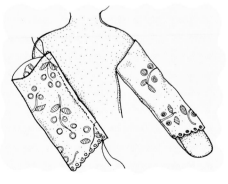

3 Stitch the two dress pieces together, right sides facing, from the bottom (raw edge) to 2½ inches (6.5cm) from the top. Turn right side out. Turn up ½ inch (1.5cm) and another ¾ inch (2cm) at the bottom edge. Topstitch.

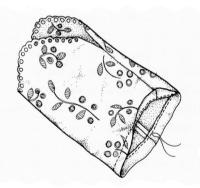

Put the dress on the doll. Turn ¼ inch (6cm) to the wrong side at arm edges. Slip stitch to the sleeves, covering the sleeves with the dress edges. At the shoulders, fold the dress front over the dress back and slip stitch in place.

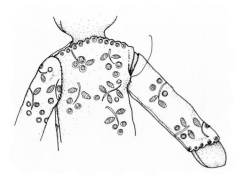

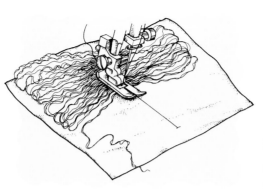

Small Dolls

Eyelet Angel

♥ 1 Cut a 3-inch (8cm) wide piece of eyelet 12 inches (30.5cm) long. Seam the two short ends, right sides together. Turn ¼ inch (6mm) to the wrong side along the top edge. Gather. Put on doll. Pull up on the stitches and knot. Hand sew to doll.

♥ 4 Cut the netting in half lengthwise so you have two 6 × 44-inch (15 × 112cm) pieces. Lay one on top of the other. Gather along the top edge through both layers. Put on the doll, overlapping the layers at the back. Pull up on the stitches and knot. Hand stitch to the doll. Tie the ribbon into a bow around the doll's waist.

♥ 7 Stitch the seam to the head. Smooth the yarn on the face side of the head to the back. Pull the yarn into a loose, low ponytail. Tie with the remaining ribbon.

♥ 8 Glue the butterfly to the doll's hair.

♥ 9 To make your doll's face, see pages 16–17.

♥ 10 Stitch the wired leaves to the doll's back. Trim extra wire. Arrange leaves.

♥ 5 Glue dried materials to the bottom edge of the dress.

Hair

♥ 6 Draw a 4-inch (10cm) long line on a piece of paper. Wind yarn back and forth across the line in 12-inch (30.5cm) lengths, filling the line thickly, machine stitching along marked line as you go. Backstitch at the beginning and end of the line. Tear the paper from the stitching.

2 Thread ribbon through the 1-inch (2.5cm) wide trim. Place around neck. Pull up on ribbon to gather the trim around neck. Tie ribbon into a bow.

3 Wind yarn back and forth to make a hank 5 inches (13cm) long. Tie a piece of yarn around the center of the yarn and knot. Stitch this knot to the top of the doll's head. Tie hair with a ribbon bow at each side of head. Glue the hair in place.

4 To make your doll's face, see pages 16–17.

5 For wings, stitch small doilies to doll's back.

Sunflower Angel

1 With right sides together, stitch the two 4½-inch (11.5cm) long edges of the dress fabric together. Turn right side out. Fold in half so the two raw edges meet and the wrong sides are together (like folding the top half of a sock cuff down). Turn ¼ inch (6mm) to the wrong side along this doubled raw edge. Gather. Place on the doll around her waist. Pull up on the stitches. Knot. Stitch to the doll to secure.

2 Fold the doily in half. Stitch or glue to the front of the doll as a collar and sleeve top. Stitch button to doily.

Hair

3 Unwind string from hair. Cut a piece 12 inches (30.5cm) long. Stitch the center piece to the center top of the doll's head. Loop each side up and tie with the string.

Wings

3 Trace the wing pattern onto the cardboard. Cut along the line. Glue the wings to the doll's back.

Star Angel

1 For dress bodice cut two pieces of fabric, each 1½ inches (4cm) square. Fold one edge ¼ inch (6mm) to the wrong side. Place this edge at the back neck and wrap top corners to front over shoulders. Glue or stitch. Repeat for front.

2 With right sides together, stitch the two 4½-inch (11.5cm) long edges of the dress fabric together. Turn right side out. Fold in half so the two raw edges meet and the wrong sides are together (like folding the top half of a sock cuff down). On the remaining raw edge turn ¼ inch (6mm) to the wrong side along this doubled raw edge. Gather. Place on the doll around her waist and over the lower edge of the bodice. Pull up on the stitches. Stitch to the doll to secure.

3 Cut two sleeves, each 2 × 3 inches (5 × 7.5cm). For each sleeve, seam the shorter ends, right sides together. Turn right side out. Put on the doll. Turn ¼ inch (6mm) to the wrong side along the shoulder edge. Gather. Stitch over the bodice fabric. Turn under ¼ inch (6mm) at the wrist edge. Gather. Stitch to wrist.

4 For face instructions, see pages 16–17.

Hair

5 Make hair as for Eyelet Angel.

Wings

6 Place a 6-inch (15cm) square of fabric face down. Lay a piece of batting on top and another 6-inch (15cm) square of fabric, this time face up, on top of that. Pin. Trace the star pattern onto the top fabric. Using a long running stitch and embroidery floss, stitch the layers together about ¼ inch (6mm) inside the traced line. Using pinking shears, cut along the line. Tack or glue the star to the doll's back.

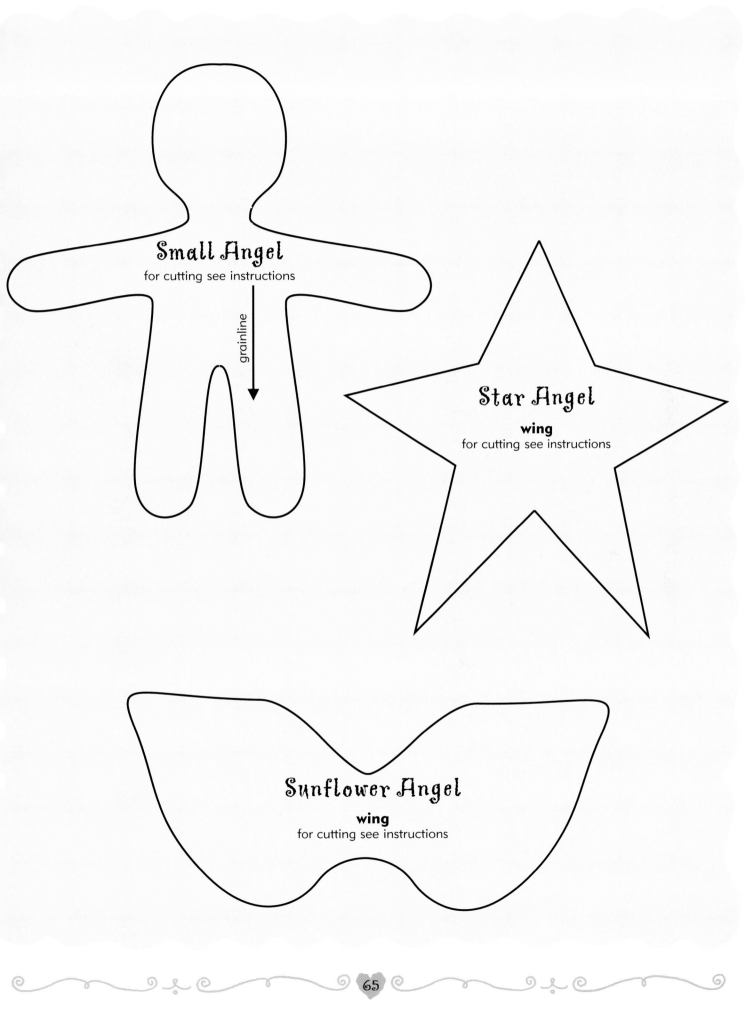

Small Angel
for cutting see instructions

grainline

Star Angel
wing
for cutting see instructions

Sunflower Angel
wing
for cutting see instructions

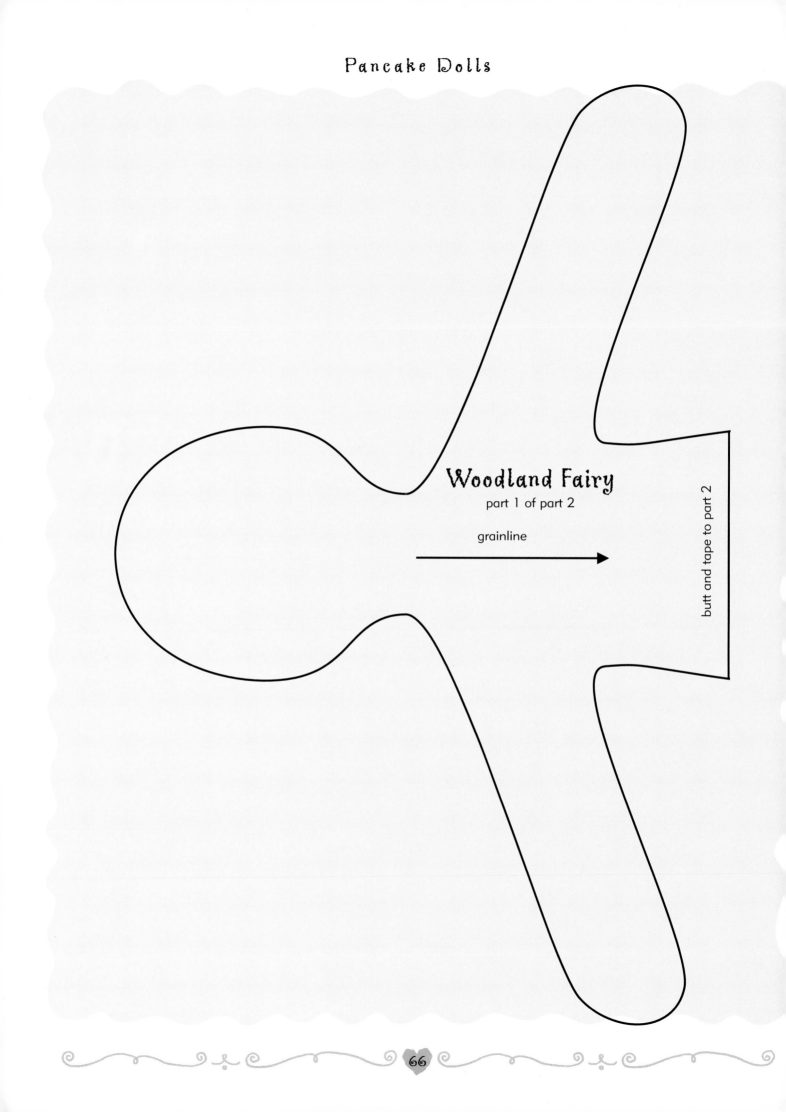

Woodland Fairy
part 1 of part 2

grainline

butt and tape to part 2

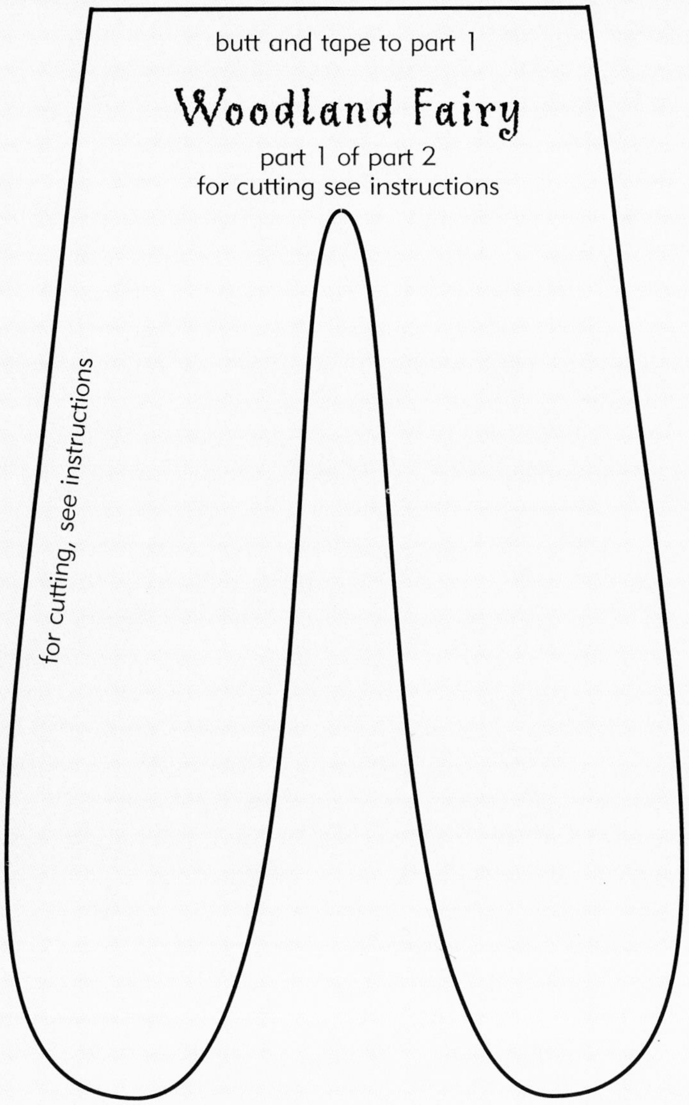

butt and tape to part 1

Woodland Fairy

part 1 of part 2
for cutting see instructions

for cutting, see instructions

Chapter eight

Christie's Christmas Angel and Friends

Finished size is 15 inches (38cm) tall.

With her arms and legs attached in a traditional cloth doll-like manner, this doll will sit and can be posed. Using just one doll body pattern and the instructions in this chapter, you can make a spectrum of elegant to whimsical angels and fairies.

materials

Doll Body:
- ♥ ½ yard (46cm) of muslin
- ♥ Matching thread
- ♥ Polyester fiberfill stuffing
- ♥ Dental floss for jointing

Christie's Christmas Angel
- ♥ ⅜ yard (34cm) of gold lamé
- ♥ ½ yard (46cm) of lace fabric
- ♥ ½ yard (46cm) of gold braid trim
- ♥ ¼ yard (23cm) of gold beaded chain
- ♥ Gold metallic machine embroidery thread
- ♥ ⅛-inch (3mm) wide elastic
- ♥ Gold yarn
- ♥ ½ yard (46cm) of muslin
- ♥ Matching threads
- ♥ Blue, gold, and red embroidery floss
- ♥ Batting
- ♥ Scrap of Wonder Under

Peggy-Lynne, The Fairy of Fun
- ♥ ¼ yard (23cm) of dress fabric
- ♥ ¼ yard (23cm) of petticoat fabric
- ♥ ⅛ yard (11.5cm) of suedelike fabric for boots
- ♥ ¼ yard (23cm) of Polar Fleece for hat
- ♥ Three ⅜-inch (9mm) buttons
- ♥ Six small buttons for boots
- ♥ Matching threads
- ♥ ⅔ yard (61cm) of 1½-inch (4cm) wide wire-edged ribbon for large rose
- ♥ ¼ yard (23cm) of 1½-inch (4cm) wide double-edged ribbon for small rose

- ♥ ¼ yard (23cm) of 1½-inch (4cm) wide double-edged ribbon for rose leaves
- ♥ 2 yards (1.8m) of 1½-inch (4cm) wide ribbon for waist tie and wings
- ♥ Chain, charm, and jump ring for necklace
- ♥ Two packages Auburn Stringlets from All Cooped Up Designs (see Sources)
- ♥ Acrylic paints

Victorian Angel
- ♥ ¼ yard (23cm) of velvet for skirt
- ♥ ¾ yard (69cm) of gold lace trim for skirt hem
- ♥ 1½ yards (1.5m) of 8-inch (20.5cm) wide organza with two finished edges for blouse and petticoat
- ♥ ¼ yard (23cm) of ¾-inch (2cm) wide gold metallic ribbon
- ♥ ⅓ yard (30cm) of ⅜-inch (9mm) wide gold metallic trim
- ♥ One ¾-inch (2cm) diameter decorative button or cameo
- ♥ ⅛ yard (11.5cm) of suedelike fabric for shoes
- ♥ ¼ yard (23cm) of gold-printed corduroy
- ♥ Four tiny buttons for shoes
- ♥ ½ yard (46cm) length of strung beads
- ♥ ½ yard (46cm) of lacy gold trim to wind with beads
- ♥ One package Dark Brown Wavy Locks from All Cooped Up Designs (see Sources)
- ♥ Matching threads
- ♥ Batting
- ♥ Acrylic paints

Raggedy Ann Angel
- ♥ ⅓ yard (30cm) of red-and-white striped fabric for legs
- ♥ ¼ yard (23cm) of fabric for dress
- ♥ ⅛-inch (3mm) wide elastic
- ♥ ¼ yard (23cm) of fabric for apron
- ♥ ⅞ yard (80cm) of eyelet fabric with one finished edge for bloomers
- ♥ ½ yard (46cm) of eyelet trim for bloomers
- ♥ ⅔ yard (61cm) of ¼-inch (6mm) wide ribbon for bloomers
- ♥ ⅛ yard (11.5cm) of black suedelike fabric for shoes
- ♥ ¼ yard (23cm) of matching ⅜-inch (9mm) wide ribbon for shoe straps
- ♥ Four small black buttons for shoes
- ♥ Two ⅜-inch (9mm) diameter buttons
- ♥ ⅓ yard (30cm) of fabric for wings and hair ties
- ♥ Batting
- ♥ 1 yard (1m) of cotton fabric for hair
- ♥ Matching threads
- ♥ Acrylic paints

instructions

Note: All seam allowances are ¼ inch (6mm) unless specified otherwise.

♥ Prepare the patterns and fabric and transfer all markings and face designs as instructed on pages 12–13.

Doll Body

2 Fold the muslin in half. Trace one body and two arms onto the muslin, leaving about ½ inch (12mm) between the patterns. Stitch along the marked lines, leaving 1-inch (2.5cm) openings at the backs of the arms as illustrated and leaving the straight edge at the bottom of the body open. Cut out doll ⅛ inch (3mm) beyond stitching. Turn right side out.

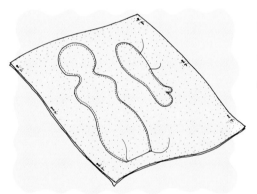

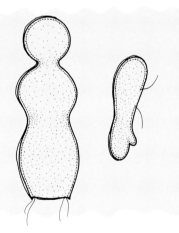

3 **For Christie's Christmas Angel:** Trace four legs onto muslin. Cut four squares of lamé, measuring approximately 6 inches (15cm). Following manufacturer's directions, fuse Wonder Under to the wrong sides of lamé

squares. Pin the squares to the unmarked sides of the muslin legs, under the shoe area of the legs. Marked side of the leg up, machine satin stitch the top edge of the shoe to the foot with gold machine embroidery thread. Repeat for the other three leg pieces and shoes. Remember to reuse the pattern for two of the legs. Trim the excess lamé above the stitching line to the satin stitching.

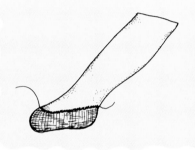

Pin pairs of leg pieces together, right sides (appliquéed shoes) facing. Stitch, leaving the straight edge at the top of the leg open. Cut out leg ⅛ inch (3mm) beyond stitching. Turn right side out.

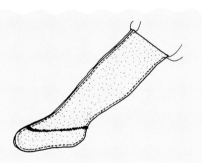

For Raggedy Ann: Fold the striped fabric in half, carefully matching the stripes. Place the leg pattern on the fabric, matching the top straight edge with a stripe. Pin. (illust 8-5) Cut out, leaving the two pieces together so the stripes will remain matched.

Stitch, leaving the straight edges at the top unstitched. Trim seam allowances to ⅛ inch (3mm). Turn right side out. Repeat for second leg.

For Victorian Angel and Peggy-Lynne: Fold the muslin in half. Trace two legs onto the muslin, leaving about ½ inch (12mm) between the patterns. Stitch, leaving the top, straight edges of the legs unstitched. Cut out legs ⅛ inch (3mm) beyond stitching. Turn right side out.

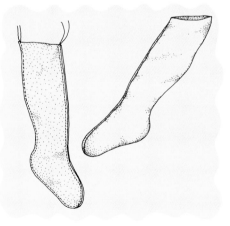

4 Stuff the head-body, paying careful attention to the neck. Turn the bottom raw edges of the body ¼ inch (6mm) to the wrong side and whipstitch the opening closed.

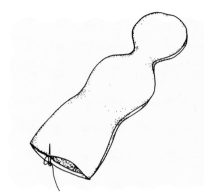

❤ Stuff arms. Ladder stitch the openings closed. Thread joint the arms to the body as instructed on page 33, or whipstitch. (For Victorian Angel, put sleeves on arms before installing arms on body; see page 52.)

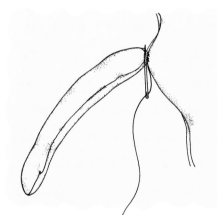

❤ Stuff the legs to within 1 inch (2.5cm) of tops. Turn the top raw edges of the legs ¼ inch (6mm) to the wrong side. Gather, pull up on the stitching, and whipstitch legs to the bottom of the body.

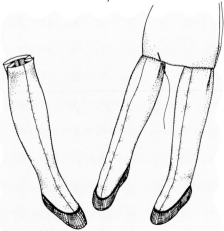

Clothing and Hair

Christie's Christmas Angel

Petticoat

❤ Cut a 16 × 18-inch (41 × 46cm) rectangle from the lace, placing one of the longer edges along the finished edge of lace.

❤ With right sides together, match the two short edges of the petticoat. Zigzag them together. Trim seam allowance close to the stitching.

To make a casing for the elastic, fold the petticoat as shown, wrong sides together, and zigzag ½ inch (12mm) from the top fold, leaving a ½ inch (12mm) opening in the stitching.

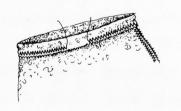

Cut a piece of elastic 6 inches (15cm) long. Attach a safety pin to one end. Insert the safety pin into the casing. Thread the safety pin through the casing and back out the opening.

Tack ends of the elastic together. Stitch the opening closed. Put the petticoat on the doll.

Robe

❤ With right sides together, stitch the robe fronts to the robe backs at shoulder-top of sleeves and at robe side-underarms.

❤ Using metallic machine thread, zigzag around all raw edges of the robe, including the bottom edges of the sleeves. Put the robe on the doll. Tie the gold braid around her waist and knot the ends.

Hair

💜5 To curl the yarn for the hair, wrap the yarn on metal skewers or metal knitting needles, securing the ends of the yarn with tape. Wet the yarn slightly. Place wrapped skewers in a 200-degree F (100-degree C) oven for 20 minutes, or until the yarn is dry. Remove from the oven. Let yarn cool and remove from the skewers. Trim off the tape.

Draw a 3-inch (7.5cm) line on a piece of paper. Lay 14 to 16-inch (36 to 41cm) long pieces of curled yarn side by side centered over the line. Machine stitch along the line, adding yarn as you go to fill the line generously. Backstitch at both ends.

Tear the paper away from the stitching. Draw a line down the center of the head starting ¾ inch (2cm) from the top of the head at the forehead and continuing down the back of the head 2¼ inches (6.5cm) as shown. Hand stitch the seam in the hair to the head along this line.

💜6 Cut a piece of gold beaded chain 7 inches (18cm) long. Butt the ends and sew them to the hair at the back of the head, about 1½ inches (4cm) down from the top point of the head. Stitch the halo to the hair at the sides of the head.

Shawl (optional)

💜7 For the shawl, cut an 8 × 24-inch (20 × 56cm) rectangle from the remaining lace fabric.

💜8 Trim the edges of the shawl along design lines. Put the shawl on the doll.

Face

💜9 Embroider the face as illustrated. Use all six strands of floss. Begin your embroidery with a knot at the back of the head and push it through to the front to begin stitching. Stitch the eyes first, then the eyebrows. After sewing each eyebrow, come up in the center of the eye and take a stitch or two with the gold thread to create a pupil. Finish with the mouth. To tie off the thread, push the needle through to the back of the head and knot it. This will be hidden by the hair.

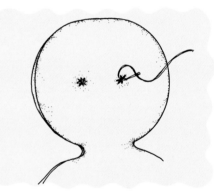

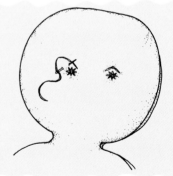

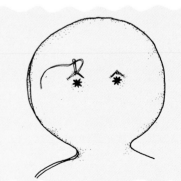

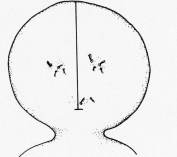

Wings

10 Cut two 16 × 20-inch (41 × 51cm) pieces of muslin. Transfer wing pattern to the right side of one piece. Lay the piece marked side down on a light box or against a sunny window. Trace the outer, wide line to the wrong (unmarked) side of the fabric. Put the two wing pieces together, right sides facing and marked piece up, and lay them on top of the batting. Stitch through all three layers, leaving a 2-inch (5cm) opening along one wing edge for turning. Cut out wings ⅛ inch (3mm) beyond stitching. Turn right side out. Press. Hand sew opening closed.

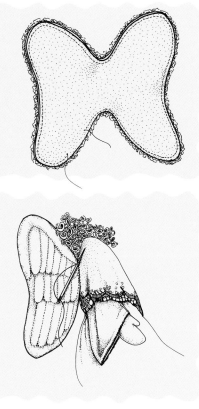

11 Machine stitch along the wing quilting lines.

12 Hand sew the wings to the doll's back.

Peggy-Lynne, The Fairy of Fun

Dress

1 With right sides together, pin one pair of bodice backs to one bodice front. Stitch together at shoulders. Repeat for lining pieces.

2 With right sides together, match and stitch the center back and neck edges of the bodice and bodice lining. Turn right side out. Press.

3 Gather along the curved edge of one sleeve top between the dots. Gather the bottom edge. Pin the sleeve to the armhole, treating the bodice and bodice lining as one. Pull up on the threads and distribute gathers evenly. Stitch. Repeat for the other sleeve top.

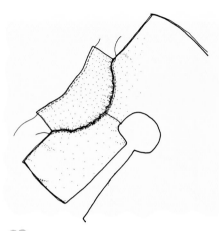

4 Pin the sleeve bottom to the sleeve top, pulling up on the stitches at the bottom of the sleeve top to fit. Stitch. Turn ¼ inch (6mm) to the wrong side on the remaining raw edge of the sleeve bottom. Topstitch. Repeat for the second sleeve.

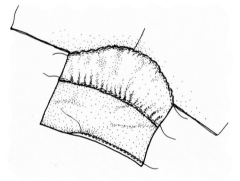

5 Stitch the underarm-side seams.

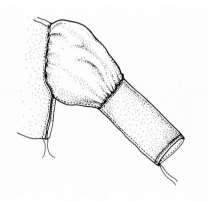

6 Fold the sleeve bottom to the wrong side until the bottom folded edge meets the top edge. Tack in place.

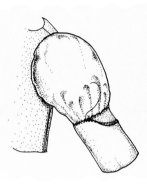

7 Cut a skirt piece 6 × 16 inches (15 × 41cm). Using a ½-inch (12mm) seam allowance, stitch the two short edges together from halfway down to the bottom. Press the seam open. Turn the raw edges of opening ¼ inch (6mm) to the wrong side. Topstitch. Gather the top edge. Press ¼ inch (6mm) twice to the wrong side along the bottom edge. Topstitch. Pin the skirt to the bodice. Pull up on the stitches to fit. Stitch.

8 Make buttonholes at markings. Try the dress on the doll. Sew buttons in place.

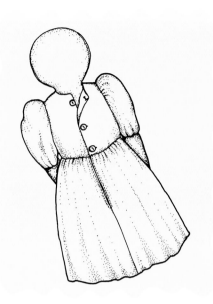

Petticoat

9 Cut a 6½ × 22-inch (16.5 × 56cm) petticoat. With right sides together, stitch the two short edges together. Press under ¼ inch (6mm) twice on one raw edge for the hem. Topstitch. Press under ¼ inch (6mm) twice on the remaining edge. Topstitch close to the bottom fold leaving a ½-inch (12mm) opening. Attach a safety pin to one end of a 6-inch (15cm) long piece of elastic. Insert into the casing and thread all the way around. Try petticoat on the doll. Tack the ends of the elastic together.

Boots

10 With right sides together, stitch two pairs of boot pieces together. Turn right side out. Put boots on the doll. Stitch buttons in place.

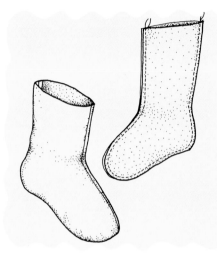

Hat

11 With right sides together, stitch two hat pieces together, leaving the bottom, straight edges unstitched. Repeat for the two remaining hat pieces. Leave a 1½-inch (4cm) wide gap in the stitching at the top of one hat (for the lining).

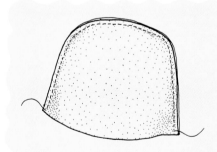

12 With right sides together, slip one hat inside the other. Stitch the straight edges together. Turn right side out through the gap at the top of one hat.

Put that hat inside the other (as a lining). Fold up the brim.

13 Make the flowers from the ribbon as illustrated below. Stitch to the hat brim as in the photo.

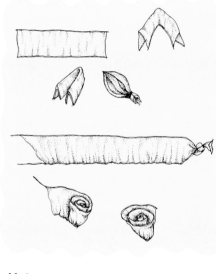

Hair

14 Put the hat on the doll. Using an air-soluble marker or light pencil, draw a line on the back and sides of the head along the bottom edge of the hat. Remove the wrapping string from the hair. Cut the hair into nine 7-inch (18cm) lengths. Fold each length in half and stitch the folds ¼ to

½ inch (6 to 12mm) above the drawn line around the head as shown.

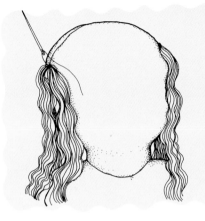

15 Put the hat back on the doll's head. Secure with a hatpin, hot glue, or tack with thread.

16 Decide how long you want your doll's necklace. Using needle-nose pliers, remove a link to shorten. Use the link to put the shortened necklace together, on the doll. Use a jump ring to attach the charm to the necklace.

Face

17 Turn to pages 16–17 for face-painting instructions.

Wings

18 Fold the ribbon into three loops for each side of the doll as shown in the photograph. Stitch to the doll's back.

Victorian Angel

Blouse

1. Cut the petticoat-sleeve-blouse fabric into four pieces: one 22 inches (56cm) long for the petticoat, one 12 inches (30.5cm) long for the blouse, and two each 10 inches (25.5cm) wide for the sleeves.

2. With right sides together, stitch the cut edges of the blouse piece together. Turn right side out. Gather ¾ inch (2cm) below one finished edge, for neck edge. Put blouse on doll. Pull up on the stitches around neck. Tie. Stitch the thinner gold ribbon over the stitches. Stitch button on top.

3. Stitch the cut edges of one sleeve together. Turn right side out. Gather 1 inch (2.5cm) from one edge, to be the bottom edge. Turn under ¼ inch (6mm) at the top edge. Gather. Pull up on the stitches. Put sleeve on arm. Stitch the gathered fabric to the inside of the arm. (Thumb points toward front.) Pull up on

stitches at wrist. Wrap thinner gold ribbon around wrist, over stitches. Hand sew in place.

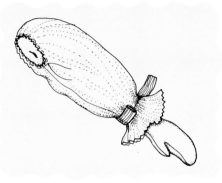

Install arm as instructed on page 34, putting the needle back through the same hole in the sleeve fabric at the outer arm.

Petticoat

4. With right sides together, stitch the cut edges of the petticoat together. Gather one long edge. Put petticoat on doll. Pull up on the stitches. Tie the ends in a secure knot.

Skirt

5. Cut the skirt fabric in half, so you have two pieces, each measuring 8 × 22 inches (20.5 × 56cm). Use one for the skirt and save the other for another project. With right sides together, stitch the short edges together. Press under ¼ inch (6mm) at one raw edge. Press under ¾ inch (2cm). Repeat for the remaining raw edge. On one of these, to be the waist edge of the skirt, machine baste. On the other, bottom edge, stitch the lace trim over the edge. Put the skirt on the doll. Pull up on the stitches at the waist. Tie securely. Hand sew the wide gold ribbon over the skirt at the waist.

Boots

6. Right sides together, stitch two pairs of boots together. Turn right side out. Put boots on doll. Stitch buttons at sides.

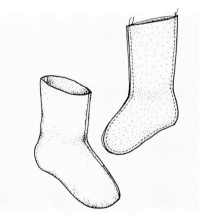

Hair

7 Loop the hair from front to back, having the folds at the hairline. Glue in place. Pull the free hair to the left side of the doll's head.

8 Twist the beads and gold trim together. Knot both ends. Anchor one knot at the left back of the head. Bring around to the front, across the front and over the hair at the back left of the doll. Wrap around the hair twice. Anchor the knot in the hair to hide it.

Face

9 Turn to pages 16–17 for face-painting instructions.

Wings

10 With right sides together, fold the wing fabric in half. Trace the wing design onto the folded fabric. Place the fabric on top of the batting. Stitch just inside the traced lines, leaving a 1-inch (2.5cm) opening along one edge for turning. Cut out wings ⅛ inch (3mm) beyond stitching. Turn right side out. Hand sew the opening closed. Hand sew the center of the wings to the doll's back.

Raggedy Ann Angel

Dress

1 With right sides together, pin and stitch the two dress pieces together at the neck-shoulder seams. Stitch the side seams from the dot down to the hem edge.

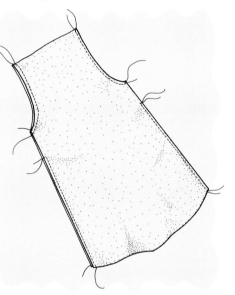

2 Press ¼ inch (6mm) to the wrong side along the neck edge. Press under 1 inch (2.5cm). Cut a piece of elastic 4½ inches (11.5cm) long. Seam the ends together with a zigzag stitch. Zigzag stitch to the bottom fold at the neck on the inside of the dress, pulling the elastic ahead of and behind the presser foot as you stitch so the elastic stretches to fit the neck edge.

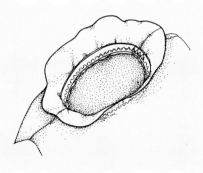

3 Press under ¼ inch (6mm) along the hem edge of the dress twice. Topstitch.

4 Gather the top edge of one sleeve between the dots. Fold so sleeve measures 4¾ × 8¼ inches (12 × 21cm). Stitch the long edges together. With right sides facing, pin the sleeve to one armhole matching the underarm seams. Adjust the gathers to fit. Pin. Stitch. Repeat for the second sleeve.

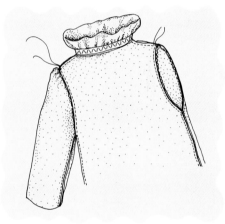

5 Press ¼ inch (6mm) to the wrong side along the hem edge of one sleeve. Press under 1 inch (2.5cm). Cut a piece of elastic 4 inches (10cm) long. Seam the ends together with a zigzag stitch. Zigzag stitch the elastic over the fold at the inside of the dress, pulling the elastic ahead of and behind the presser foot as you stitch so the elastic stretches to fit. Repeat for the second sleeve.

Apron

6 With right sides together, pin two bodice backs to one bodice front. Stitch at shoulders. Repeat for the second set; these will be the lining.

7 With right sides together, pin the bodice to the bodice lining. Stitch at back and neck edges and at armholes. Turn right side out. Press.

8 With right sides together, stitch the lining and bodice side seams as one. Press.

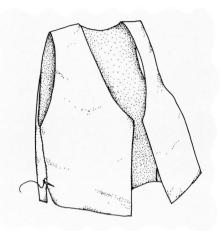

9 Cut a skirt 6¼ × 20 inches (16 × 51cm). Press ¼ inch (6mm) twice to the wrong side along both short edges of the skirt. Topstitch. Repeat for one long raw edge, which will be the hem.

10 Gather the remaining raw edge of the skirt. Pin to one layer of the bodice, right sides facing, pulling up on the stitches to fit. Stitch. Fold ¼ inch (6mm) under along the raw edge of the free (lining) bodice. Pin and slip stitch in place.

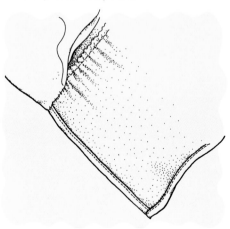

11 Make buttonholes as marked on the bodice back. Stitch buttons in place.

Bloomers

12 With right sides together, stitch the inside leg seams of both legs.

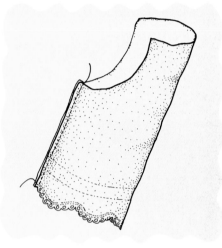

13 Turn one leg right side out. Slip inside the other. Match and stitch the crotch seam.

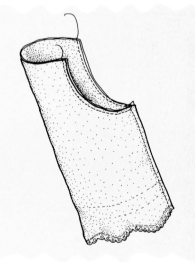

14 Press under ¼ inch (6mm) along the top edge. Press under ⅜ inch (9mm). Topstitch close to the bottom fold, leaving a ½-inch (12mm) opening in the stitching. Cut a piece of elastic about 10 inches (25.5cm) long. Attach a safety pin to one end of the elastic. Insert into the casing through the gap in the stitching and thread the elastic around and back out the opening. Try bloomers on the doll. Trim elastic to fit plus ½ inch (12mm). Remove from doll. Overlap the ends ¼ inch (6mm). Stitch together. Stitch the gap in the stitching closed.

15 Topstitch the top and bottom edges of the trim to the bloomer legs, about 2 inches (5cm) from the bottom. Overlap the ends, turning the raw end under. Thread the ribbon through the eyelets. Put the bloomers on the doll. Tie the ribbons in bows, gathering the bloomer legs. Trim excess ribbon.

Shoes

16 With right sides together, stitch two shoe pieces together. Repeat for lining, leaving a ¾-inch (2cm) opening in the stitching along the bottom for turning.

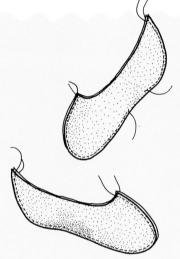

17 Turn the shoe lining piece right side out. Slip inside the shoe. Stitch the top raw edges together. Turn right side out. Stitch the opening in lining closed.

18 Put the shoe on the doll. Cut a piece of black ribbon to extend across the front of the shoe and about ¼ inch (6mm) down the sides of the shoe. Tack to the shoe with the buttons. Repeat for the second shoe.

Hair

19 Trim the selvage edges from the hair fabric. Cut or tear into strips measuring ¼ inch (6mm) wide along the shorter length of the fabric. Group the pieces together and cut in half. Stitch down the center of the strips, distributing them so they measure about 6½ inches (16.5cm). Draw a

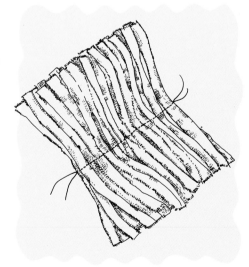

line across the doll's head about ½ inch (12mm) in front of the head seam. Hand stitch the machine stitching of the hair to the line. Smooth

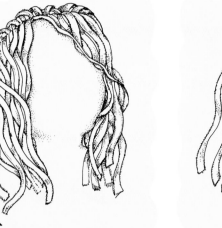

the hair to the back. Pull hair from the sides to the back and tie with the strip of hair fabric. Trim excess tie fabric.

Face

20 Turn to pages 16–17 for face-painting instructions.

Wings

21 With right sides together, fold the wing fabric in half. Trace the wing pattern onto the fabric. Place fabric on top of two or more layers of regular quilt batting. Stitch just inside the marked lines, leaving a 1-inch (2.5cm) opening along one edge for turning. Cut out wings ⅛ inch (3mm) beyond stitching. Turn right side out. Hand sew the opening closed. Hand sew the center of the wings to the doll.

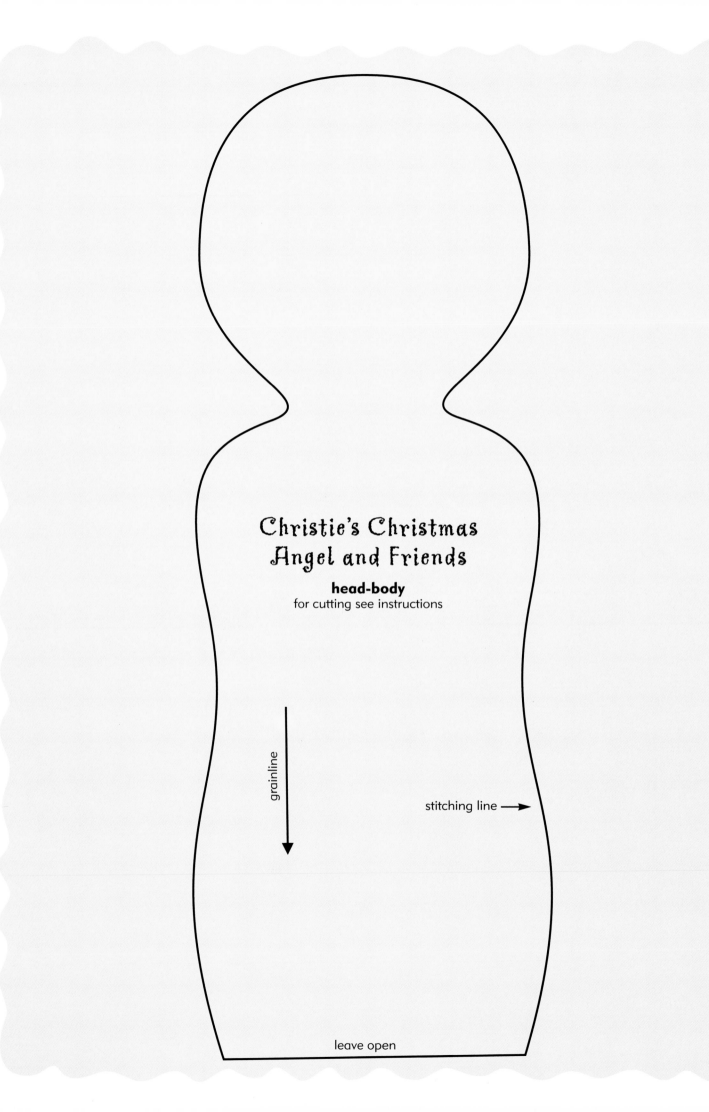

Christie's Christmas
Angel and Friends

head-body
for cutting see instructions

grainline

stitching line →

leave open

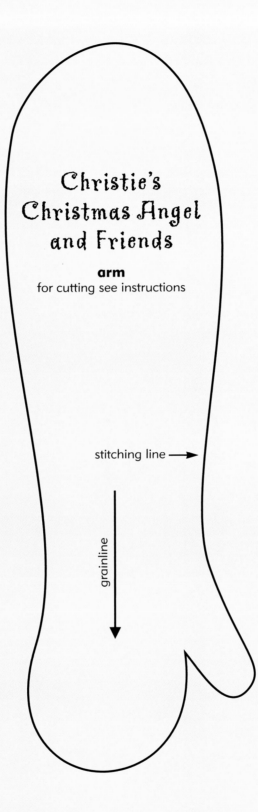

Christie's
Christmas Angel
and Friends

arm
for cutting see instructions

stitching line ⟶

grainline

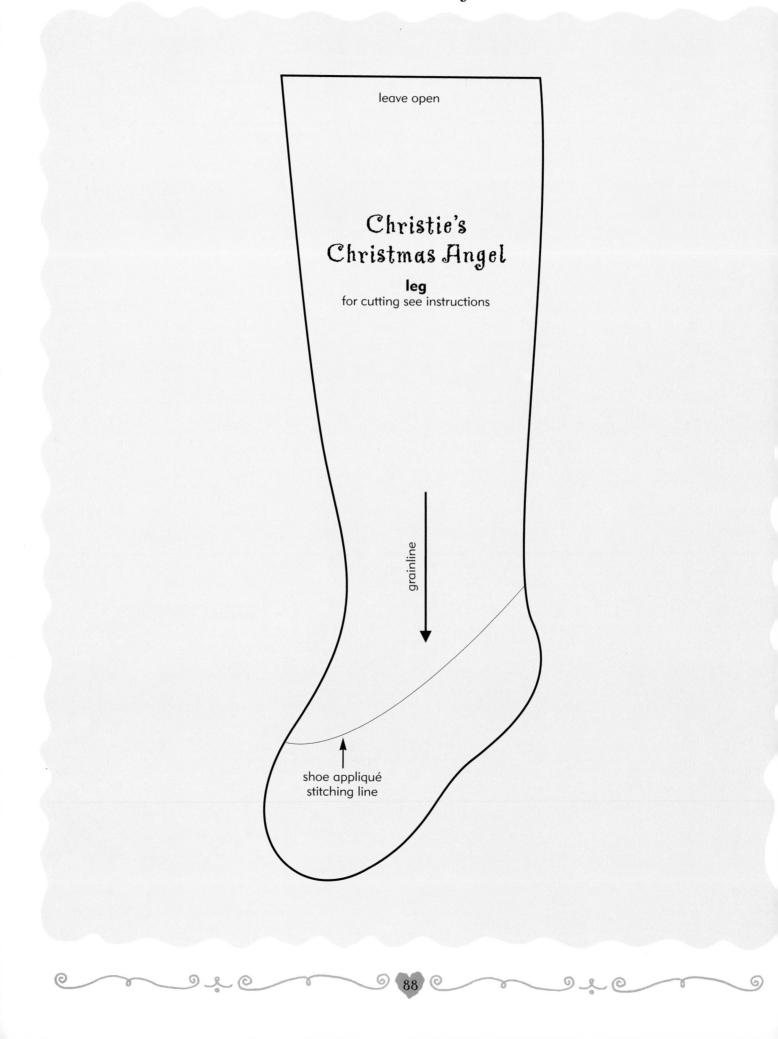

leave open

Christie's
Christmas Angel

leg
for cutting see instructions

grainline

shoe appliqué
stitching line

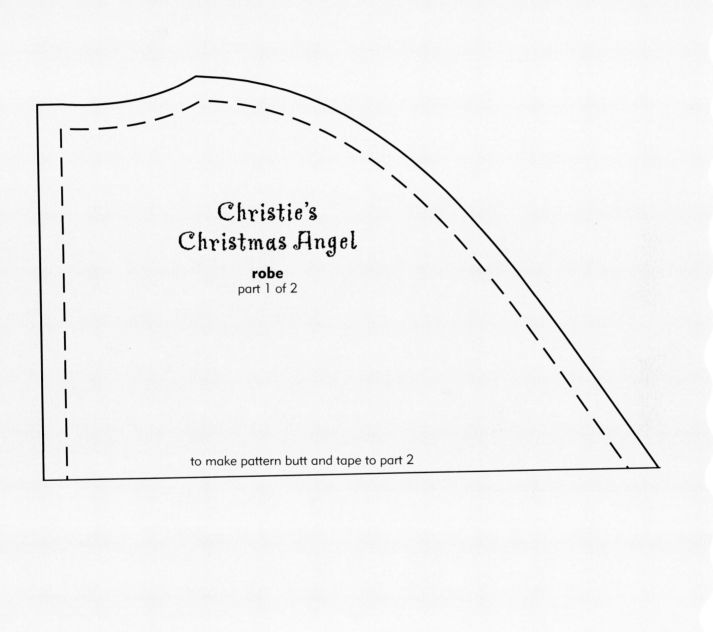

Christie's
Christmas Angel

robe
part 1 of 2

to make pattern butt and tape to part 2

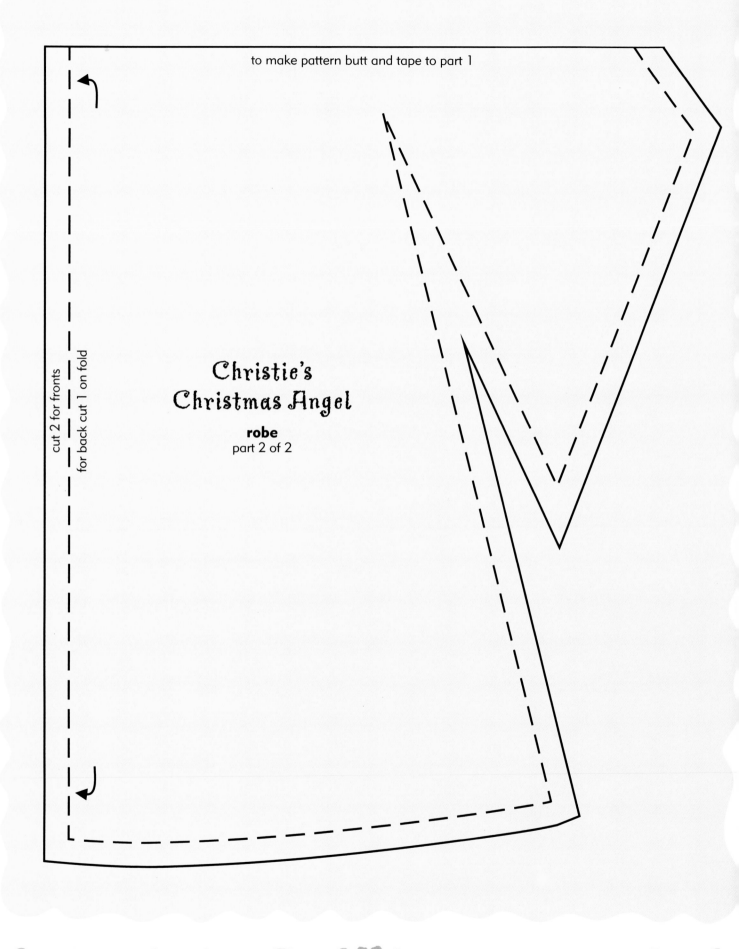

to make pattern butt and tape to part 1

Christie's
Christmas Angel

robe
part 2 of 2

cut 2 for fronts

for back cut 1 on fold

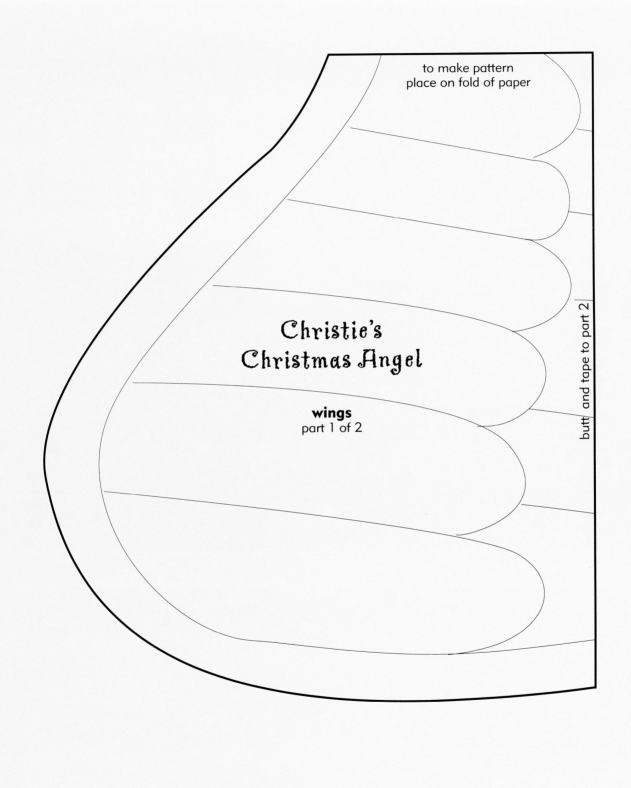

to make pattern
place on fold of paper

Christie's
Christmas Angel

wings
part 1 of 2

butt and tape to part 2

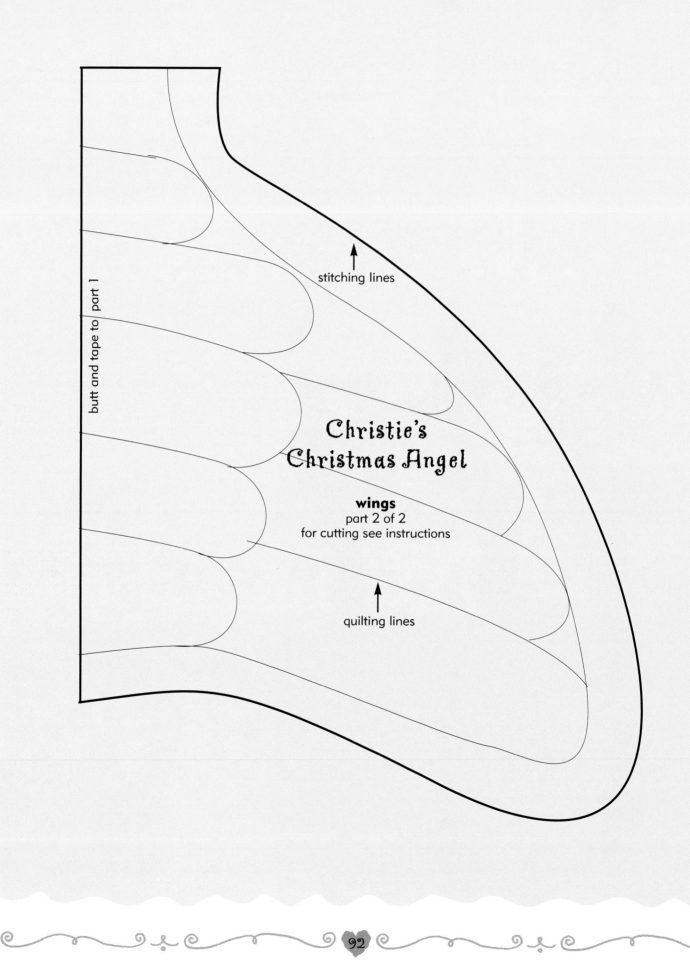

butt and tape to part 1

stitching lines

Christie's
Christmas Angel

wings
part 2 of 2
for cutting see instructions

quilting lines

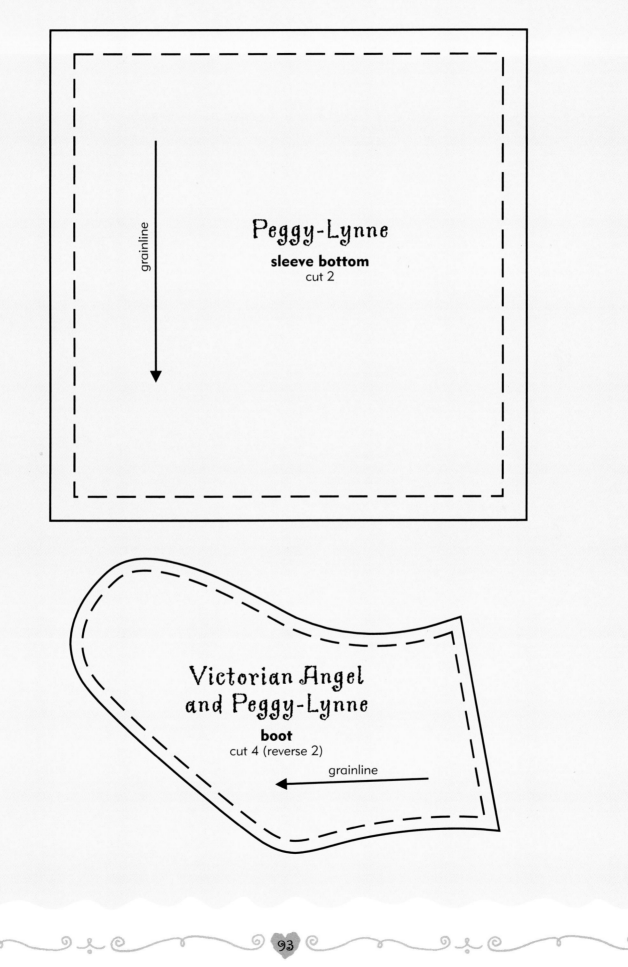

Peggy-Lynne

sleeve bottom
cut 2

grainline

**Victorian Angel
and Peggy-Lynne**

boot
cut 4 (reverse 2)

grainline

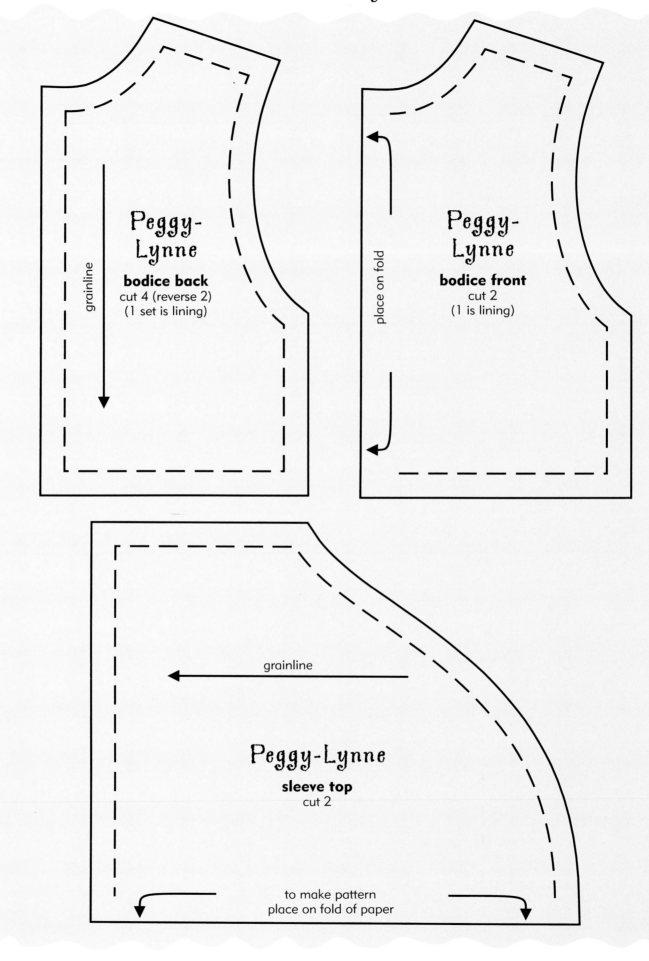

Peggy-Lynne

bodice back
cut 4 (reverse 2)
(1 set is lining)

grainline

Peggy-Lynne

bodice front
cut 2
(1 is lining)

place on fold

Peggy-Lynne

sleeve top
cut 2

grainline

to make pattern
place on fold of paper

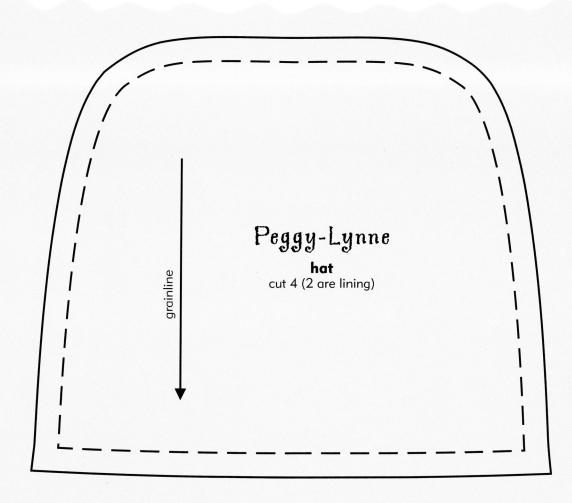

Peggy-Lynne

hat
cut 4 (2 are lining)

grainline

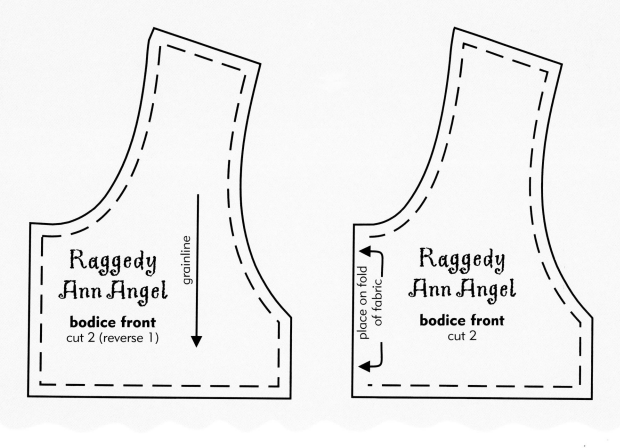

Raggedy
Ann Angel

bodice front
cut 2 (reverse 1)

grainline

Raggedy
Ann Angel

bodice front
cut 2

place on fold
of fabric

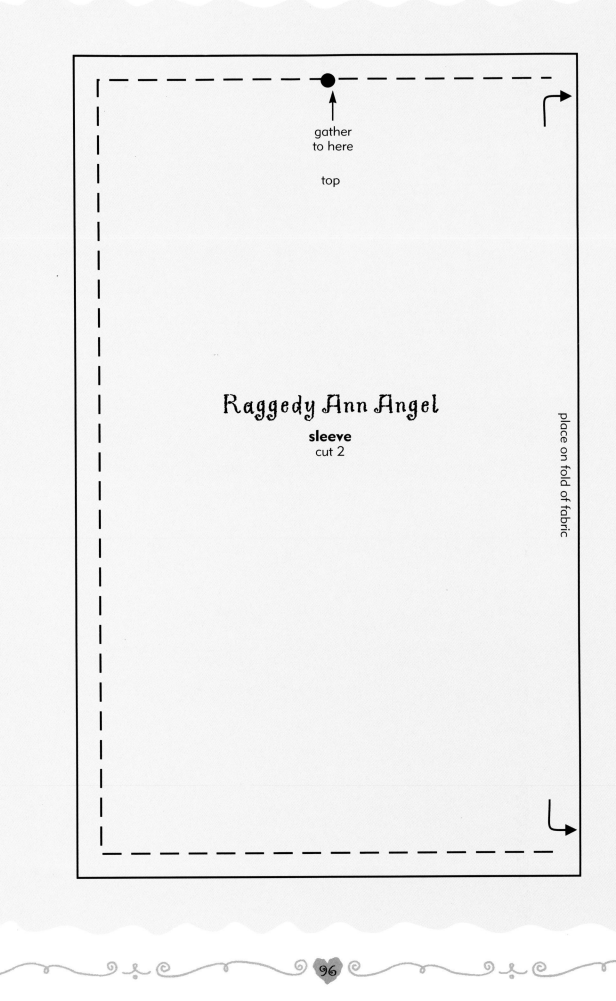

gather
to here

top

Raggedy Ann Angel

sleeve
cut 2

place on fold of fabric

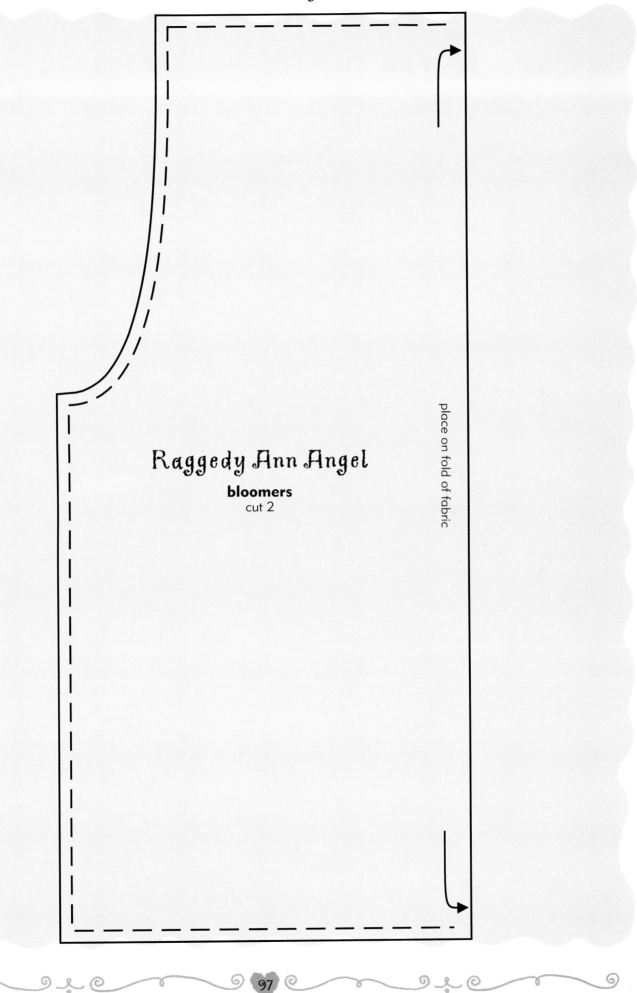

place on fold of fabric

Raggedy Ann Angel

bloomers
cut 2

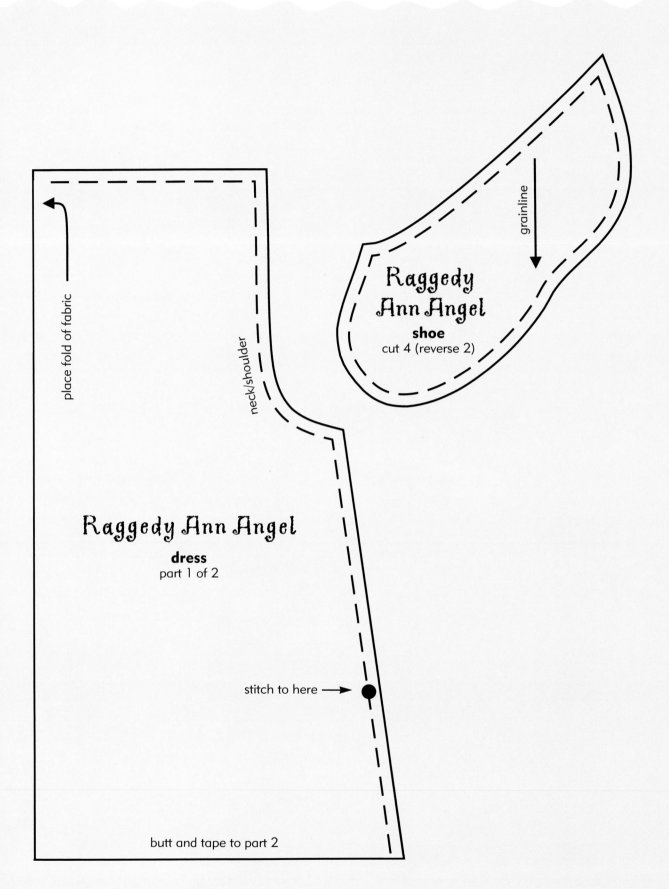

place fold of fabric

neck/shoulder

grainline

Raggedy
Ann Angel

shoe
cut 4 (reverse 2)

Raggedy Ann Angel

dress
part 1 of 2

stitch to here →

butt and tape to part 2

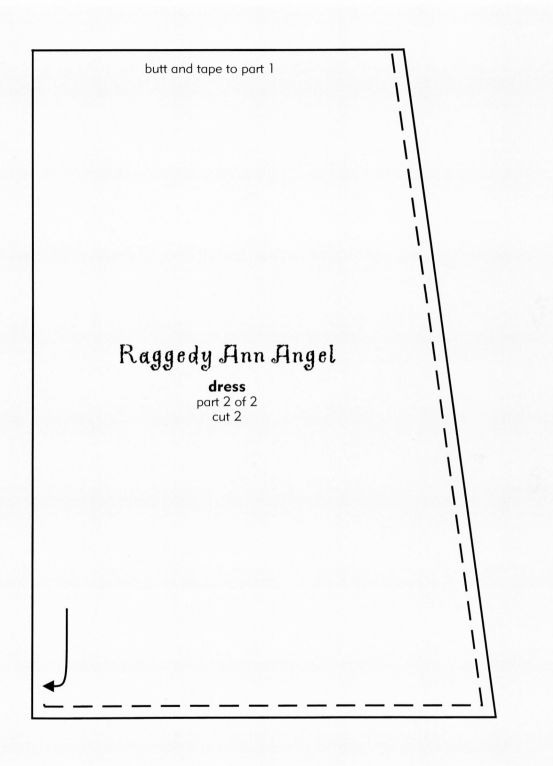

butt and tape to part 1

Raggedy Ann Angel

dress
part 2 of 2
cut 2

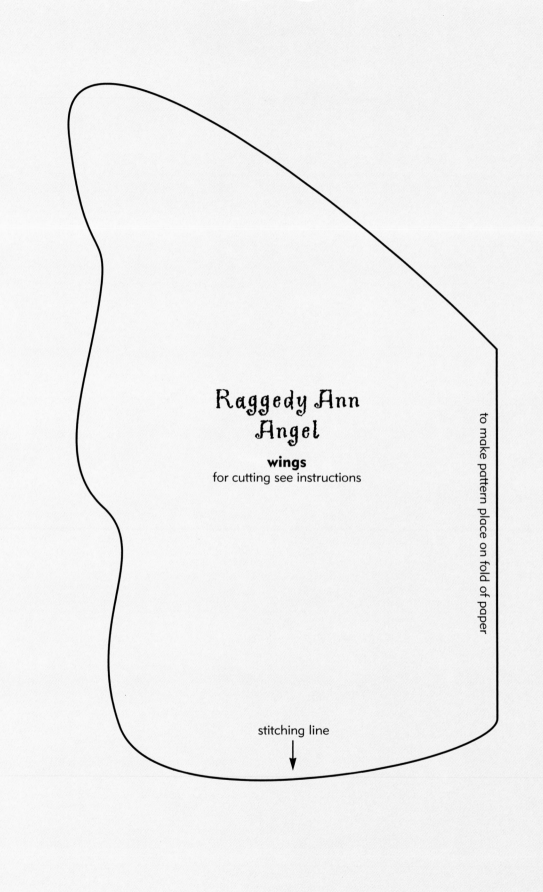

Raggedy Ann
Angel

wings
for cutting see instructions

to make pattern place on fold of paper

stitching line

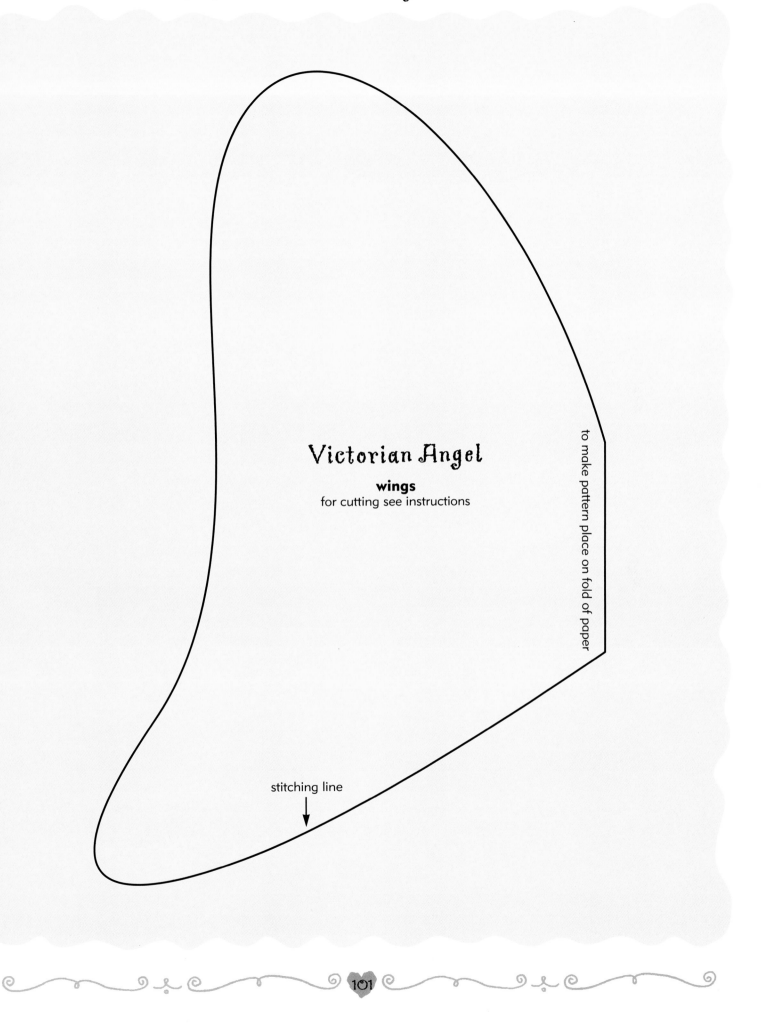

Victorian Angel

wings
for cutting see instructions

to make pattern place on fold of paper

stitching line

Chapter nine

More Angels and Friends

Finished size is 14 inches (35.5cm) tall.

More challenging than the other dolls in this book, this pattern can be made into three lovely angels. I found some wonderful imported lace in a New Hampshire shop for my Edwardian Angel. The crinkly gold and iridescent purple-gold fabric for the Harvest Angel came from the same store. Her crown is a purchased candle wreath, although it would be easy to craft one. The Fairy Godmother's curly tresses are a wig.

materials

Body

- ¼ yard (23cm) of muslin
- Matching thread
- Polyester fiberfill stuffing
- Waxed dental floss

Edwardian Angel

- ⅓ yard (30cm) of fabric for underdress
- ⅓ yard (30cm) of 6-inch (15cm) wide lace
- ½ yard (46cm) of 3-inch (7.5cm) wide lace
- Matching threads
- Gold paint
- ⅔ yard (61cm) of ¼-inch (12.6cm) wide ribbon for hair
- ½ yard (46cm) of ⅝–1-inch (1.5–2.5cm) wide ribbon for shoes
- Six tiny buttons or beads
- One package Dark Brown Curly Locks from All Cooped Up Designs (see Sources)
- Purchased Wings

Fairy Godmother

- ⅓ yard (46cm) of satin
- Matching thread
- 1⅝ yard (1.5m) of lace fabric with a finished edge
- 1¾ yard (1.6m) of 1-inch (2.5cm) wide ribbon
- Two small feather fans (found in bridal department of crafts stores)

- Gold wire
- Gold star button or charm
- ⅛ yard (11.5cm) of strung pearls

Harvest Angel

- ¼ yard (23cm) of fabric for underdress
- ⅔ yard (61cm) of 6-inch (15cm) wide gathered lace
- Matching threads
- ½ yard (46cm) of 2-inch (5cm) wide wire-edged metallic ribbon
- ½ yard (46cm) of 1-inch (2.5cm) wide wire-edged metallic ribbon
- ⅛ yard (11.5cm) of strung faux pearls
- ½ yard (46cm) of gold crinkled fabric
- Paint
- Honey Natural Fiber Tresses from By Hand... (see Sources)
- Wreath for hair
- Fabric stiffener (by Aileene's, or Stiffy brand)

instructions

Note: All seam allowances are ¼ inch (6mm) unless specified otherwise.

❤ 1 Prepare the fabrics and patterns as instructed on page 12.

Body

❤ 2 Trace the patterns onto the body fabric, leaving ½ inch (12mm) or more between the pieces. Do not cut out.

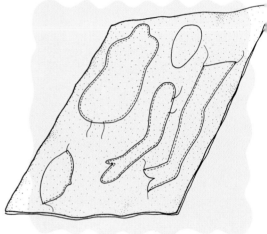

❤ 3 Machine stitch just inside the marked lines for the arms, leaving a ¾-inch (2cm) opening at the top back of the arms for turning and stuffing. Cut out arms ⅛ inch (3mm) beyond stitching. Apply seam sealant to the seam allowances at the openings. Allow to dry. Turn arms right side out.

❤ 4 Stitch the front and back of the legs from the top to the bottom, just inside the marked lines. Cut out the legs ⅛ inch (3mm) beyond stitching. Cut along the marked lines at the top of the leg and the toes. Match the raw edges at the toes, lining up the front and back seams. Stitch, using a ⅛-inch (3mm) seam allowance. Turn right side out.

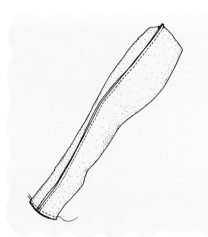

Whipstitch leg to the bottom of the body. Repeat for the second leg.

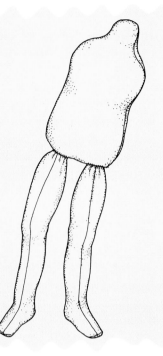

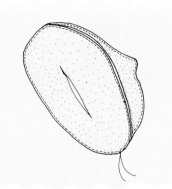

Apply seam sealant to edges of slit. When dry, turn right side out. Stuff. Whipstitch the opening closed. Stitch the back bottom of the head to the neck securely.

5 Stitch the body, leaving a 1½-inch (4cm) wide opening at the bottom for turning. Cut out the body ⅛ inch (3mm) beyond stitching. Apply seam sealant to the seam allowances at the opening. Allow to dry. Turn body right side out.

6 Stuff the legs, body, and arms.

7 Hand stitch the openings in the body and the arms closed.

8 Turn ¼ inch (6mm) to the wrong side along the top of one leg. Gather the top edge of the leg, treating the two layers as one.

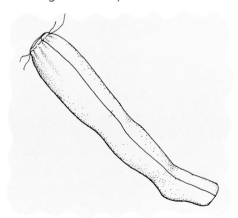

9 Stitch the center front head seam from top to bottom, just inside the marked line. Trim the seam allowance to ⅛ inch (3mm). Cut head out along the remaining marked line. Cut the head back along the marked line. With right sides together, pin the head front to the head back. Stitch, using a ⅛-inch (3mm) seam allowance. Make a slit at the back of the head.

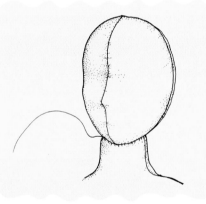

10 Refer to the doll instructions to apply sleeves. Install the arms by following the thread jointing instructions on page 33. Leave the outside of the sleeve free. For the Harvest Angel, thread joint the arms before dressing the doll.

Clothing

Edwardian Angel

💜 Cut a 9½ × 16-inch (24 × 40.5cm) piece of fabric for underdress. With right sides together, seam the two short edges together. Along one raw edge turn the raw edge ¼ inch (6mm) to the wrong side for hem. Zigzag along the fold. For added decoration use a contrasting or metallic thread. Trim fabric close to the stitching. Along remaining raw edge, turn ¼ inch (6mm) to the wrong side. Gather. Put the underdress on the doll. With the top folded edge even with the tops of the shoulders, pull up on the stitches to fit. Hand sew in place.

💜 Zigzag the two cut edges of the 6-inch (15cm) wide skirt lace together. Gather along the top edge. Put on the doll. Pull up on the stitches. Knot the thread. Hand sew the lace to the waist of the doll.

💜 Cut the 3-inch (8cm) wide lace into three pieces: one 9 inches (23cm) wide for the bodice and two 4½ inches (11.5cm) wide for the sleeves. Wrap the bodice around the body, having it extend over the top of the skirt. Overlap the raw edges at center back. Turn one raw edge under ¼ inch (6mm) and stitch to the back of the doll, covering the other raw edge. Stitch in place.

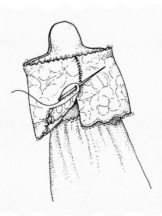

💜 Seam the cut edge of each sleeve together. Gather the top edge and put on the arm. Thread joint the arms to the doll's body.

💜 Paint slippers onto the doll's feet. When dry, stitch ribbon bows to shoes.

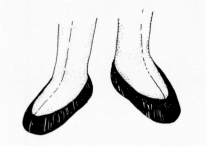

💜 Draw a 3-inch (7.5cm) long line on a piece of paper. Lay the centers of 12-inch (30.5cm) long sections of hair along the line and perpendicular to it. Machine stitch along the line. Hand sew this "part" to the doll's head around the front hairline. Pull the hair to the back of the head. Wrap a piece of ribbon around the hair and tie in a bow high at the back of the doll's head.

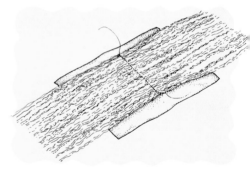

💜 Hand sew the wings to the doll's back.

Fairy Godmother

💙 Cut a 4 × 6½-inch (10 × 16.5cm) piece of satin for the bodice. Turn one long edge of the bodice top ¼ inch (6mm) to the wrong side. Wrap around doll's torso as shown. At center back lap one raw edge over the other, turning under ¼ inch (6mm). Slip stitch center back and top edge to doll.

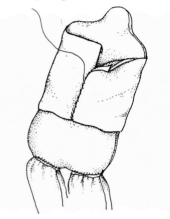

💙 Cut a 10 × 18-inch (25 × 46cm) piece of satin for the skirt. With right sides together, stitch the short edges of the skirt together. On one remaining raw edge fold ¼ inch (6mm) to the wrong side twice. Topstitch. On the remaining raw edge fold ¼ inch (6mm) to the wrong side twice. Gather. Place on doll. Pull up the stitches to fit doll's waist. Knot. Hand sew to doll.

💙 From the unfinished edge of the lace, cut a 4 × 6½-inch (10 × 16.5cm) piece. Turn the top, raw edge ¼ inch (6mm) to the wrong side. Hand sew to doll over the satin bodice.

💙 With right sides together, stitch sleeve seams, leaving the straight bottom edges open. Press under ¼ inch (6mm) twice at the lower edge. Topstitch. With right sides facing, stitch two sleeves together. Turn both sleeves right side out. Put satin sleeve inside lace sleeve. Put sleeve on doll's arm. Install arm as instructed on page 52.

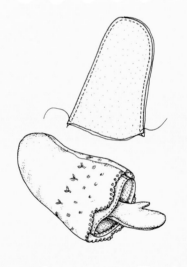

💙 Cut two 8 × 10-inch (20.5 × 25cm) pieces of lace, with one long edge along finished edge of lace. Stitch the short edges of one piece together. Place the second piece over and around the first, so both right sides are facing up and the 10-inch (25cm) raw edges of the second piece meet at the center front of the bottom piece, which is directly opposite the seam. Gather along one long raw edge. Put on the doll. Pull up on the stitches. Knot. Hand sew to the doll.

Cut a 10-inch (25cm) long piece of lace fabric. Fold the long raw edges to the inside. Tie around the doll over the stitching, making a knot at the back waist.

Tack the loose ends of the lace fabric to the underside of the knot. Turn the outer lace skirt under and up at each corner at the front. Tack.

💙 Stitch pearls to the doll's neck.

7 Draw a 3½-inch (9cm) line on a piece of paper. Lay 8-inch (20.5cm) long pieces of hair over the line, having the centers along the line. Stitch the yarn to the paper, backstitching at each end and adding hair as you go to fill the line. Tear the paper away from the stitching.

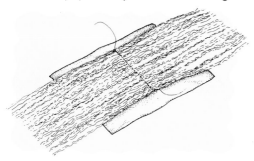

Hand sew the machine stitching to the doll's head, about ¼ inch (6mm) in front of the side head seam, from just below one ear, over the head, to just below the other. Pull the hair in front of the face to the back and tie with a scrap of ribbon.

8 Thread two gold wires through the loops of the buttons. Place buttons at center of wire. Fold wire at buttons. Twist wires together or glue the gold charm to the end of the wire. Stitch to doll's hands.

9 Glue or stitch the two feather fans to the back of the doll.

Harvest Angel

1 Cut a 4 × 6½-inch (10 × 16.5cm) piece of fabric for bodice. Fold one long edge of the bodice piece ¼ inch (6mm) to the wrong side. Put on the doll as shown, wrapping it around to the back. Pin along the top edge at the front. Fold one center back edge under ¼ inch (6mm). Slipstitch along back at top edges.

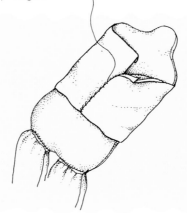

2 Cut an 8½ × 12-inch (22 × 30.5cm) underskirt. With right sides together, stitch the short edges of the underskirt together. Fold under ¼ inch (6mm) along one raw edge. Baste. Fold under ¼ inch (6mm) on the remaining edge. Satin stitch along the fold. Trim the extra fabric close to the stitching.

Cut the skirt lace into three 12-inch (30.5cm) pieces. Seam the cut edges of each piece together. Stitch one piece, for the bottom tier, 1¼ inch (3cm) below the top edge of the skirt, wrong side of lace facing right side of skirt. Position the second tier

halfway between the bottom tier and the top edge of the skirt. Stitch the top tier along the top edge of the skirt. Machine baste on top of this stitching to gather the skirt. Put the skirt on the doll. Pull up on the stitches. Knot thread. Hand sew the top skirt edge to the doll.

3 Twist the beads and narrower ribbon together. Stitch to the front top edge of the bodice. The ends will be hidden by the overdress.

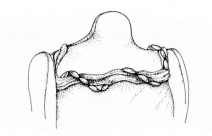

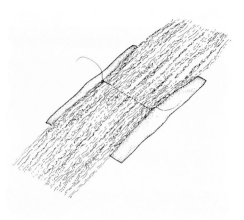

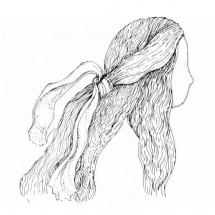

💜 4 Cut two 5½ × 18-inch (14 × 46cm) pieces of the crinkled over-dress fabric. Drape each over one shoulder having pieces overlap at the back and tucking the fronts under the arms, as shown. Twist the ribbon and put around the waist, gathering the overdress under the arms and tying the ribbon at the back.

the line. Tear the paper away from the hair. Place the hair on the doll's head so the stitching (the "part") runs from front to back. Hand stitch to the head. Pull the top front sections of hair loosely to the back. Tie with scraps of gold crinkled fabric. Tack the wreath to the doll's head.

💜 7 Cut the gold crinkled fabric into three 1 × 18-inch (2.5 × 46cm) strips. Taper the ends into soft points. One strip at a time, apply fabric stiffener to fabric following manufacturer's directions. Twist into soft twists. Pin strips to waxed paper to dry. When dry, group centers of strips and stitch to the doll's back.

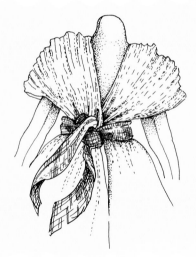

💜 5 Paint the slippers. Make two bows with the remaining narrow ribbon. Stitch bows to the fronts of the slippers.

💜 6 Draw a 2½-inch (6.5cm) line on a piece of paper. Lay 10-inch (25cm) long pieces of hair across line, having centers on the line. Stitch, backstitching at the beginning and end of the line and adding hair as you go to fill

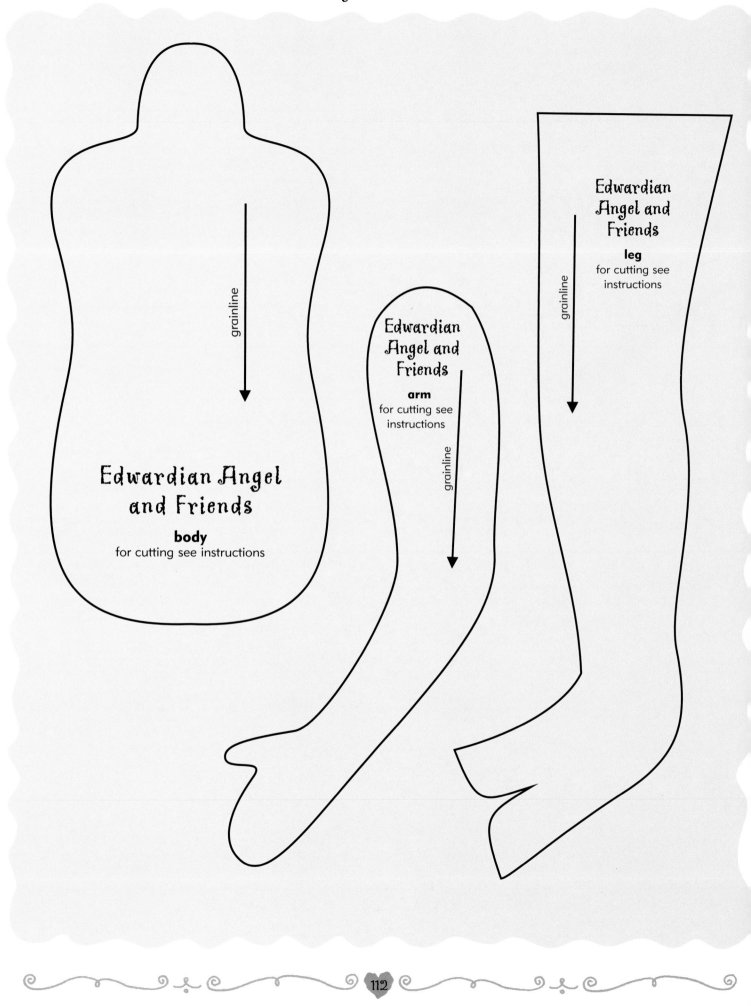

Edwardian Angel
and Friends

body
for cutting see instructions

grainline

Edwardian
Angel and
Friends

arm
for cutting see
instructions

grainline

Edwardian
Angel and
Friends

leg
for cutting see
instructions

grainline

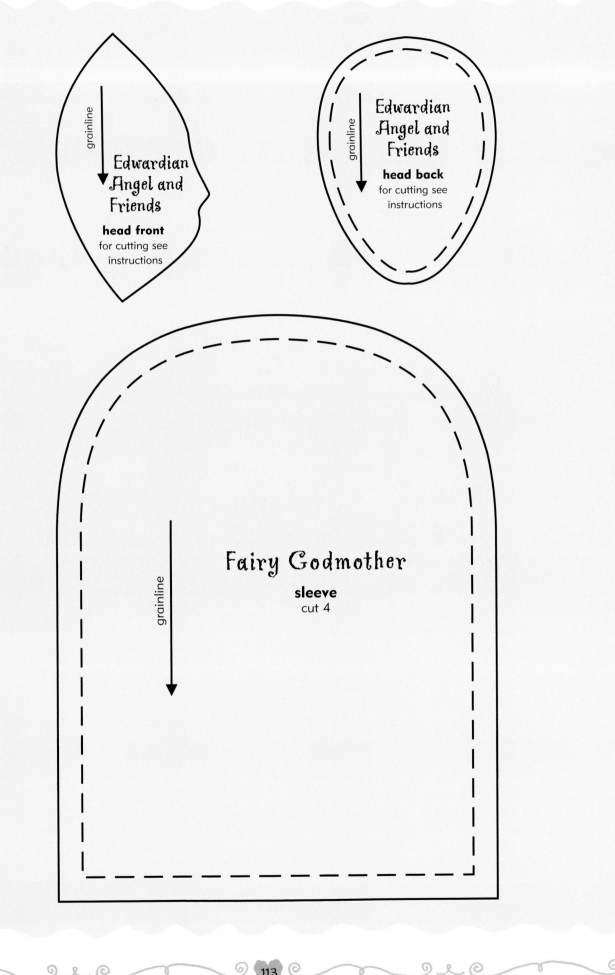

grainline

Edwardian Angel and Friends

head front
for cutting see
instructions

grainline

Edwardian Angel and Friends

head back
for cutting see
instructions

grainline

Fairy Godmother

sleeve
cut 4

Chapter ten

Bear Angel

Finished size is 6½ inches (16.5cm) tall.

Standing a mere 6½ inches (16.5cm) tall, this bear angel is the perfect size to adorn a Christmas wreath or tree, or to sit in a favorite spot to bring cheer any time of year.

When choosing fur fabric for your bear, take into account his diminutive size. A ¼-inch (3mm) pile mohair or synthetic fur (see Sources), upholstery velvet, and velveteen are just the right scale.

materials

- ♥ ¼ yard (23cm) of fabric for bear
- ♥ Matching thread
- ♥ Two 5mm glass eyes (see Sources) or beads
- ♥ Polyester fiberfill stuffing
- ♥ Waxed dental floss or carpet thread
- ♥ Dollmaker's needle for jointing
- ♥ Perle cotton or embroidery floss
- ♥ Gold covered wire for halo
- ♥ ½ yard (46cm) of ribbon
- ♥ White dove for wings

instructions

Note: All seam allowances are ⅛ inch (3mm).

1 Prepare the pattern as instructed on page 12. To cut the fur, find the nap of the fur by stroking it as you would a dog. Lay the fabric with the nap pointing toward you and the backing side up, flat on a table. Line up all of the pattern pieces on the fur with their arrows pointing toward you, with the nap of the fur toward the dog's tail. The arrows will then be aligned with the grain of the backing. Trace around the pattern pieces with an air-soluable pen.

Cut a single layer of fur at a time. Make small snips with your shears, cutting only through the backing, not the fur pile. Cut just inside the traced lines. Cut the required number of each pattern piece, flipping to reverse them if indicated on the patterns. Transfer all markings to the backing. Transfer the markings to the right side of the fur by taking a stitch from the right side of the fur through the center of the dot, leaving tails of colored thread on the fur side.

2 Pin the two body pieces with right sides together. Stitch, using a ⅛-inch (3mm) seam allowance and leaving an opening between the dots at the back for turning and stuffing. Turn the body right side out.

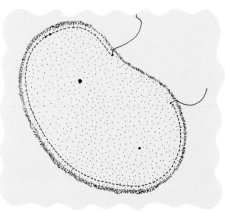

3 Fold the arm in half, so the fur sides are together. Match the raw edges of the arm all the way around. Pin. Using a ⅛-inch (3mm) seam allowance, stitch all the way around arm, leaving the space between the dots at the top of the arm open for turning and stuffing. Repeat for the second arm. Turn the arms right side out.

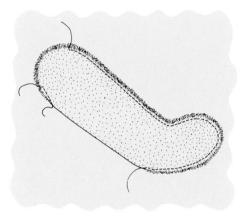

Tip: To facilitate turning tiny body parts, insert a hemostat into the limb, grabbing a far bit of the fabric and pulling the body part right side out. Go slowly and use great care.

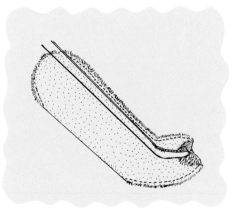

4 Fold one leg in half with the right sides together. Stitch, leaving an opening between the dots for turning. Repeat for the second leg.

5 Pin the foot pads to the bottoms of the feet, right sides together. Match the large dot on the foot pad to the front leg seam and the small dot to the back leg seam. Stitch. Turn the legs right side out.

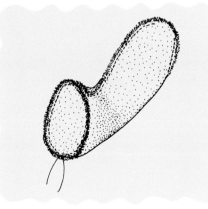

6 Pin the two side head pieces together, right sides facing, from the nose to the base of the neck. Stitch.

7 Pin the dot on the head gusset to the seam where the two head pieces meet at the tip of the nose. Pin one side of the gusset from the tip of the nose to the base of the neck, easing the gusset to fit as you go. Stitch. Repeat for the other side. Turn right side out.

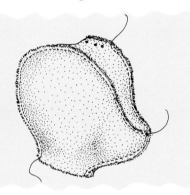

8 Match two ear pieces, right sides together. Stitch the rounded edges together, leaving the bottom edges open. Turn. Turn 1/8 inch (3mm) to the inside at the bottom raw edges. Whipstitch closed. Repeat for the second ear.

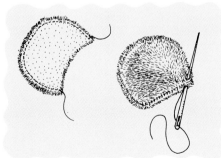

9 Stuff the head. Using dental floss or doubled thread, hand baste along the bottom, neck edge of the head. Pull up on the stitches tightly. Baste around one more time. Pull up on the basting again. Secure with a knot.

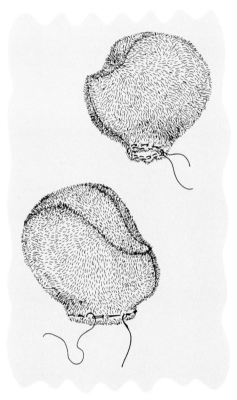

10 To install the glass eyes, cut the wire with wire cutters about ¾-inch (2mm) from each eye. Bend the last third of the wire back on itself and bend it down again.

Experiment with eye positions by pushing two pins into the head and repositioning them until you are happy with their placement. With small scissors, an awl, or a seam ripper, make holes at the pins for the eyes. Thread

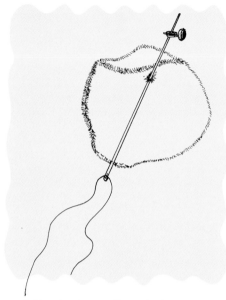

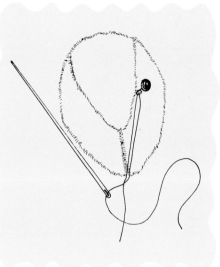

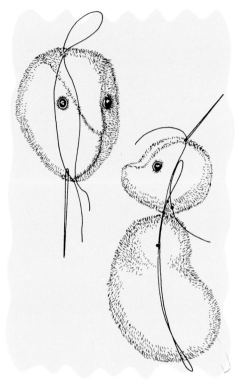

a dollmaker's needle with dental floss. Push it through the bottom of the bear's head and come out through the eye hole. It will take a few stabs to get the needle to come out exactly in the hole.

Put the needle through the loop in the eye wire (or, if the needle is too large for the hole in the loop, just work the thread onto the loop as you would if linking one paper clip to another) and push the needle back into the hole from which it just emerged.

Push the needle out through the base of the neck. Pull the thread very tightly, seating the eye flatly and firmly against the head. Pull again to be sure the eye is secure.

Make a stitch in the fabric at the bottom of the neck to secure the thread. Push the needle back into the bottom of the neck and out through the second eye hole. Put the eye on the thread as above, go back in through the eye hole, and emerge at the base of the neck. Make sure both eyes are firmly seated and that the wire shanks are inside the head before knotting the thread.

🐻 Stuff the arms, legs, and body. Ladder stitch (see page 15) all openings closed.

🐻 To joint the head, insert the needle into the base of the neck and then out the center top of the head. Go back into the head in the same hole the needle just emerged from and out the bottom. Push the needle into the top of the body and out the bottom. Go back into the same hole at

the bottom of the body, through the neck, and out the top of the head. Pull the thread tight. Go back in the same hole at the top of the head and out the bottom of the body. Pull tight again. Make a knot in the thread an inch or two from where it emerges from the bear. Insert the needle into the hole you just emerged from and out anywhere on the bear's body. Pull tight, popping the knot into the bear's body, thereby anchoring the knot in the body. Go back into the hole the needle just emerged from, then emerge anywhere. Trim the thread close to the fur.

🐻 Install the arms and legs in the same manner.

💙 **14** Decide where you want the ears. Pin them in place. Stitch them to the head in a circular motion, sewing through the ear at the top of the circle and the head on the bottom of the circle.

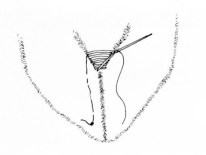

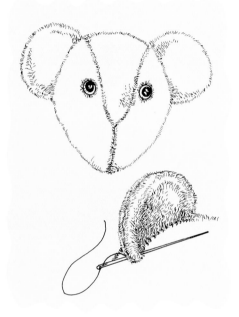

💙 **15** To embroider the nose and mouth, thread a needle with the embroidery floss or perle cotton. Knot one end. Center the template over the chin seam, having the top of the template even with the gusset seam.

Push the needle into the bear at the base of the head, hiding the knot under the neck. Emerge to the left-hand side of the top of the nose. Pull up on the thread, seating the knot. Push the needle into the top right-hand point of the nose and out at the left side, just below the first stitch. Continue in this manner until you have completed the nose.

After the last stitch, come out at the center bottom of the nose. Push the needle into the fabric at the left-hand corner of the mouth, about 3/8 inch (9mm) below the nose and 3/8 inch (9mm) to the left of the chin seam. Bring the needle out of the fabric on the seamline and about 1/2 inch (12mm) along the chin seam below the nose so that it runs between the thread and the left corner of the mouth. Push the needle back into the fabric at the right side of the mouth

and out through the neck. Make a knot, hiding it in the bear's neck.

💙 **16** Bend one end of the wire into a circular shape, about 2 inches (5cm) in diameter. Bend the remainder of the wire down, at right angles to the circle. Wrap the end of the wire around the bear's neck. Trim any extra wire. Tie the ribbon into a bow around the bear's neck, covering the wire.

💙 **17** Cut the wings from the dove. Glue wings to the bear's back.

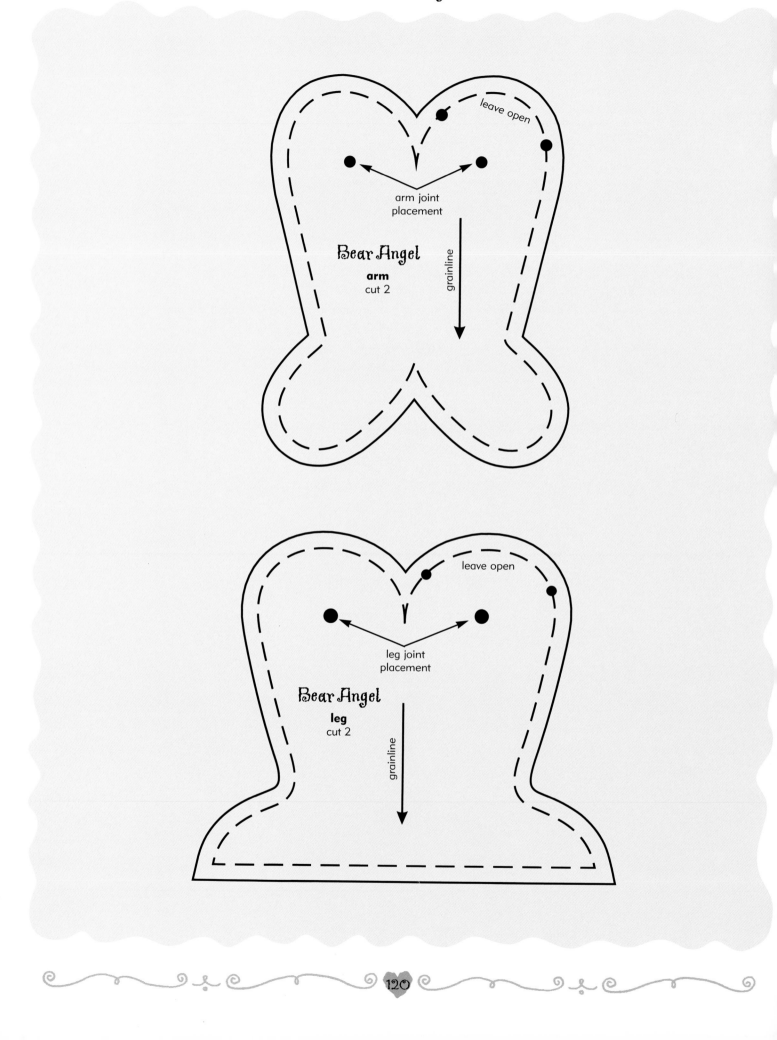

leave open

arm joint
placement

Bear Angel

arm
cut 2

grainline

leg joint
placement

leave open

Bear Angel

leg
cut 2

grainline

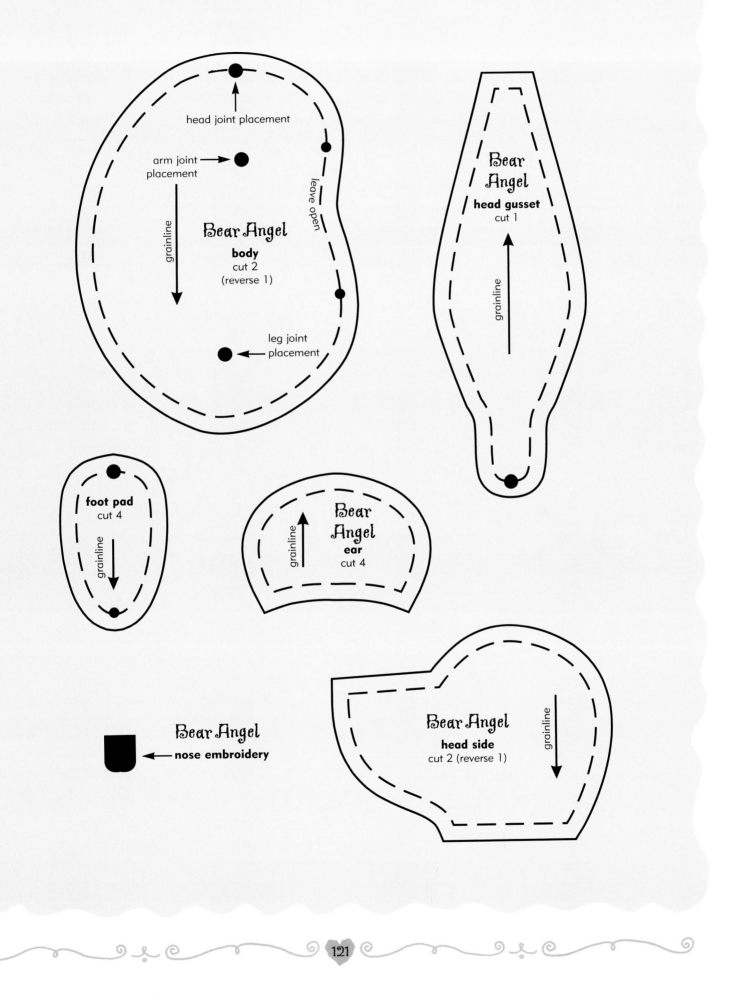

head joint placement

arm joint placement

grainline

Bear Angel
body
cut 2
(reverse 1)

leave open

leg joint placement

Bear Angel
head gusset
cut 1

grainline

foot pad
cut 4

grainline

Bear Angel
ear
cut 4

grainline

Bear Angel
nose embroidery

Bear Angel
head side
cut 2 (reverse 1)

grainline

You Are Invited...

I find the most pleasurable element of a dollmaking
class—besides the utter magic of creating the dolls themselves—
is the camaraderie of the students. Swapping ideas
and making new friendships compound the joy manyfold.

With this in mind, I invite you to share the joy of
dollmaking through the mail. Send photos and letters
describing your dolls and dollmaking to me at the address below.
Whether you use my patterns "as is," modify them, choose
different materials, or strike off with your own designs,
I will enjoy meeting you and your dolls.

Jodie Davis

Jodie Davis Publishing, Inc.
15 West 26th Street, New York, NY 10010

or via e-mail:
CompuServe: 73522,2430

Sources

All Cooped Up Designs
934 N. Industrial Park Drive
Orem, UT 84057
(801) 226-1517

Many of the angels are wigged with hair and doll wigs from this company, like the Karin wig I used for the Fairy Godmother. The hair is widely available from fabric and crafts stores and through mail-order sources. Contact the company if you have trouble obtaining its products.

By Hand...
A Division of Classic Elite Yarns
12 Perkins Street
Lowell, MA 01854

If you can't find By Hand... doll hair locally, contact the company for mail-order information.

Connecting Threads
5750 N.E. Hassalo
Portland, OR 97213
(800) 574-6454
Catalog: Free

Quilting and related books, including a few on dollmaking.

CR's Crafts
Box 8
Leland, IA 50453
Catalog: $2.00 ($4.00 Canada, $7.00 other countries)

Great prices and a wide selection of doll-and teddy bear–making supplies as well as general crafts supplies make this a must-have catalog. Carries dollmaking needles, a good selection of doilies in a variety of shapes, sizes, and styles as well as many types of doll hair, including those by All Cooped Up Designs.

Dick Blick
P.O. Box 1267
Galesburg, IL 61401
(800) 723-2787
Catalog: Free

Find Pigma pens; colored pencils, pens, and fabric markers; the Prismacolor marker, and more for your doll faces in this huge art materials catalog.

Edinburgh Imports, Inc.
P.O. Box 722
Woodland Hills, CA 91365-0722
1-800-EDINBRG
Catalog: Two first-class stamps

Wonderful selection of everything you need for bear making, including furs, eyes, and patterns. Inquire about samples of their delightful imported furs.

Home-Sew
P.O. Box 4099
Bethlehem, PA 18018
Catalog: Free

This small catalog features a variety of laces and elastics, plus basic sewing supplies at great prices.

Keepsake Quilting
Route 25B
P.O. Box 1618
Centre Harbor, NH 03226-1618
(800) 865-9458
Catalog: Free ($1.00 for first-class mail)

Along with an excellent selection of quilting supplies, you'll find patterns, books, the Stuff-It tool, Pigma pens, and quality muslin for doll bodies. For doll clothing, send for the swatch samples of cotton fabrics.

Nancy's Notions
P.O. Box 683
Beaver Dam, WI 53916-0683
(800) 245-5116
Fax: (800) 255-8119
Catalog: Free

Nancy carries every sewing notion imaginable, including Pigma Micron pens for doll faces.

Patterncrafts
P.O. Box 25639
Colorado Springs, CO 80936-5639

A color catalog full of doll and stuffed animal patterns. Carries the Stuff-It tool, dollmaker's needles, hemostats, and All Cooped Up Designs doll hair.

Sax Arts and Crafts
P.O. Box 5170
New Berlin, WI 53151
(800) 558-6696
Catalog: Free

Sax carries Pigma pens, Prismacolor markers, and all sorts of doll face-making supplies, as well as a comprehensive array of art supplies.

Twice As Nice
3811 Douglas Avenue
Des Moines, IA 50310
(515) 279-0849

Available in many quilting shops, Twice As Nice yarns were used in a number of the angels in the book. If you have trouble locating Twice As Nice doll hair, contact the company.

Wimpole Street Creations
P.O. Box 395
West Bountiful, UT 84087
(801) 298-0504
Many of the doilies I used as wings and clothing are from this company, and are widely available from both large and small craft stores. If you have trouble obtaining doilies, contact Wimpole Street Creations and they will direct you to a source.

Bibliography

Books

Bailey, Elinor Peace. *Mother Plays with Dolls.* McLean, Va.: EPM Publications, Inc., 1990.

————. *The Rag Doll.* Saddle Brook, N.J.: Quilt House, 1994.

Cely, Antonette. *Cloth Dollmaking.* This self-published three-ring binder is an excellent advanced text. Her dolls are convincingly lifelike. For information write to Antonette at 3692 Cherokee Road, Atlanta, GA 30340-2749.

Davis, Jodie. *Easy-to-Make Cloth Dolls and All The Trimmings.* Charlotte, Vt.: Williamson Publishing, 1990.

————. *Easy-to-Make Fairy Tale Characters.* Charlotte, Vt.: Williamson Publishing, 1990.

————. *Teach Yourself Cloth Dollmaking.* New York, N.Y.: Friedman/Fairfax Publishers, 1995.

Dodge, Venus A. *The Dolls Dressmaker.* New York, N.Y.: Sterling Publishing, Inc., 1991.

Gourley, Miriam. *Cloth Dolls: How To Make Them.* Gualala, Calif.: The Quilt Digest Press, 1991.

Magazines

The Cloth Doll
P.O. Box 2167
Lake Oswego, OR 97035
(503) 244-3539
Fax: (503) 244-2370

Index

Index